SOCIAL SUPPORT:
A Reflection of Humanity

Edited by
John D. Morgan, Ph.D.

Death, Value and Meaning Series
Series Editor: John D. Morgan

Baywood Publishing Company, Inc.
AMITYVILLE, NEW YORK

Library of Congress Catalog Number: 2001037800
ISBN: 0-89503-259-7 (cloth)
ISBN: 0-89503-261-9 (paper)

Library of Congress Cataloging-in-Publication Data

Social support : a reflection of humanity / edited by John D. Morgan.
p. cm. - - (Death, value, and meaning series)
Includes bibliographical references and index.
ISBN 0-89503-259-7 (cloth) - - ISBN 0-89503-261-9 (pbk.)
1. Grief therapy. 2. Social networks. I. Morgan, John D., 1933- II. Series.

RC455.4.L67 S65 2001
616.89'14- -dc21

2001037800

Preface

Rabbi Earl Grollman, D.H.L., D.D.

When those who have sustained a significant loss are asked, "What hurts the most?" a most frequent response is "I'm so alone and lonely." They may have lost a confidante, ally, lover, protector as well as one to nurture. C. S. Lewis eloquently describes this feeling: "Her absence is like the sky, spread over everything."

Dying and death are an assault on the meaning of life itself. Loneliness is an essential component of the complex emotion of mourning. It is the longing for a past that cannot be retrieved, the part that was invested and reciprocated in measure. This gaping hole—this painful state—is a verification of what each one meant to the other. How then to manage wisely the deprivation of the inner-security of the grief-stricken?

Since the publication in 1959 of Herman Feifel's volume, *The Meaning of Death*, research into the intricate area of dying and death has burgeoned. What has been lacking is a comprehensive resource which would provide the latest conceptual dynamics and practical guidance for social support.

Editor John D. Morgan has assembled this essential reference for those who accompany the devastated lonely. The contents contain a "who's who" list with a one-of-a-kind source book. Each author offers a well-balanced overview of the significant theories and skills written from the vantage point of his or her vast expertise.

This collection, more than the sum of its parts, has a unique cohesiveness that brings the reader full circle in the exploration of every aspect of positive reinforcement. Included are the philosophical roots of social support, holistic approaches for the dying patient, the role of religious faith and spirituality, help for grieving children and teenagers, strategies for potential suicides, unique gender pathways, and assistance for the caregivers experiencing their own feelings of grief in settings of death and tragedy. And there is much more.

When even breathing becomes a monumental task for the bereaved, this long overdue book sheds a light of hope to those who minister to the dying and bereaved. There is an additional challenge. Each of us must become involved with the larger world of the other lonely who suffer the ills of unemployment, homelessness, divorce, and mental illness. This need is called in Hebrew, *Tikkun Olam*, to help repair the world by creating *communities of caregivers.*

"Each of us is a once-in-the-life of the universe," Jack Morgan reminds us. There is no greater need than for the caregivers to remember this statement when they work with those who are lost in their own private world of grief. In their loneliness, they can't comprehend how anyone can relate to their anguish. When caregivers pierce the armor of their isolation, they receive an unexpected bonus. Not only do they feel enriched, needed, and important but they gain new perspectives in their own individual lives. There is the often asked query: "How can you do this work?" The response is almost universally the same: "We get more out of it than we give."

The closing sentence of Thorton Wilder's Pulitzer Prize classic *The Bridge of San Luis Rey* contains the beautiful prose: "There is a land of the living and a land of the dead and the bridge is love, the only survivor, the only meaning." In each page of this volume is the thrust of love—that the lonely may make it but they need not do it alone. That is why social support is essential to grief reconciliation. For in truth, love multiplies by division.

Table of Contents

Introduction

John D. Morgan, Ph.D.

Social Support is the name of the game. As I have read helping literature through my career as a teacher, university administrator, and program organizer, I have realized the truth of the fact that we cope with the many issues we have to face in life because of our own personality, and because of the social support that we have available. While some of the research might indicate that personality is a more important predictor of stress or bereavement outcome, the fact is if we are going to address any of the limits of our personality, we need social support. We need social support to achieve whatever we are going to achieve in this life. "No human being is an island unto self."

Human persons build walls around themselves. None of us could survive in the workplace, in the community, often even in our homes, if we allowed everyone to see how truly vulnerable we are. Those of us who work with the dying and bereaved are privileged to be with other persons when they take the chance to remove a few walls from their protection, when they dare to be themselves. Because they make themselves vulnerable, they deserve the best that we have to offer. It is our hope in presenting this book that they will be better served.

When I asked my colleagues to prepare chapters for this book, I emphasized that the book was to be practical, not theoretical. While some of the authors might be known for the teaching and writing they have done in the field of Thanatology, this book is written from their practical experiences as counselors and facilitators. I think that we have produced a very useful book.

I wish to express my appreciation to Baywood Publishing Company, especially its President Mr. Stuart Cohen, for the support that they continue to offer to the Death Education/Death Awareness community. By making these books available to the helping community they have advanced the learning that is necessary to continue our work.

CHAPTER 1

Social Support and Human Nature

John D. Morgan

And the Lord said, It is not good for man to be alone (Genesis, 2, 18).

Examining the nature of social support brings us face-to-face with fundamental questions about what it is to be human. In our individualistic, post-Existentialist thinking, we have become quite conscious of our individuality. We believe that never before in the history of the universe did any one of us exist, never again will we exist, at least in the same way. "Each of us is a once-in-the-lifetime-of-the-universe event" [1, p. 12]. We feel independent. Our culture encourages us to be independent.

The difficulty is that independence fails us when we are under stress or in a crisis situation, when "our environment is *appraised* as taxing or exceeding our resources" [2, p. 27]. We need to rely on others. Does our reliance on another person indicate a fundamental flaw in our nature, or is it a clue about what being human really is?

In this chapter, I wish to examine the foundations of social support. Why are we social? Why do we need to be supported? Why do we need to give support?

THE SOCIAL NATURE OF THE HUMAN PERSON

There have been several answers to the question of why persons are social. Perhaps the most famous is that of Thomas Hobbes, the eighteenth century political philosopher. Hobbes believed that human beings are not fundamentally social, rather the very nature of the person is self-seeking. Each person acts solely for his/her own interest. In theory, all persons are equal. The weakness that one person has in one area (physical strength, for example) is compensated for by strength in another. In practice, some will always be stronger than others. As a result, one is on guard all the time and ". . . the life of man is solitary, poor, nasty, brutish and short" [3, p. 107]. To counteract this fundamentally dangerous situation, people developed societies for mutual protection. Hobbes advocated a strong government in which everyone would surrender rights to a sovereign so that each person would do as little damage as possible to another. According to Hobbes, one cannot expect a peaceful society outside of a strong, oppressive government, a government made necessary by the selfish and violent nature of the person.

Not everyone agrees that the nature of the person is fundamentally violent. While Jean-Jacques Rousseau agreed with Hobbes that the social nature of the human person is an arbitrary construct, he also believed that all individuals are intrinsically good. In Rousseau's terms human beings were "born free," but always found in chains [4, p. 291]. Outside of a social construct, we are "noble savages." Society or government enchains persons by interfering with one's best instincts. However, since we all fear the aggression caused by the unenlightened, we urge even stronger governments, which further enchain us.

Each of these two versions of the social contract theory starts with the assumption that society is an unnatural construct, perhaps a necessary evil, in which individuals surrender their rights for the sake of mutual protection; the best of a bad situation. Both Hobbes and Rousseau accept the assumption that everyone forfeits something in order to be a part of the society. The reasoning is that it is better to have a few defended rights than an unlimited number of undefended ones. The effect of such an assumption is that when one sees the limitations that exist in all socio-political systems, one may believe that he/she has given up too much to protect the rights of the few that do not include him/herself.

There is another view that for centuries was called the natural law theory. This ancient view, rooted in the thought of Plato and Aristotle, holds that every good thing that we have is a result of society. The person is naturally social. Individuals are in society and have obligations to society because they cannot be fully human outside of society [5]. In society, which is a natural organization, one gives up nothing because one never had the unlimited rights viewed by either Hobbes or Rousseau.

I believe that the natural law theory, the thought of Plato, Aristotle, Augustine, Aquinas, and the majority of thinkers throughout the 2500-year history of Western thought, is the root of contemporary ideas about social support. We support one another, and we seek support from one another, because we believe that it is truly human to do so. While we may think that we are isolated beings, the reality is that we are beings-in-connection. As Dale Larson stated it:

> This view says that as a species we are "prewired" to be cooperative, helpful, and altruistic; that we are programmed to be our brother's keeper. It proclaims

> that there is a hero in us all, that compassion and caring are part of the fabric of human existence, and that human nature is essentially good and constructive [6, p. 12].

I am impressed with how much the students with whom I work are committed to working with others, to being available to others. In some cases they have come to take seriously their fundamental pro-social nature because of the losses in their own lives: "I often notice that caregivers who have known grief in their lives are more likely to 'go the extra mile' for other grieving persons" [6, p. 13]. In other cases, students seem always to have been aware of their connectedness to others: "their feeling of responsibility for the welfare of others, including those outside their immediate familial or communal circles" [6, p. 19].

It is not surprising that humans have developed the capacity for being in relation and for recognizing that they are in relation. There were other animals that were larger and more aggressive than our ancestors. Our ancestors no doubt discovered that they would survive only if they worked in unison. Survival meant being in relationship. Even today, thriving in the home or the workplace requires cooperation. "In many ways, our very sense of ourselves is connected to our ability to negotiate the world of friendship" [2, p. 168]. How often do we hear about colleagues who have great talent, but lack "people skills"? "The individual [is] a constellation or community of semi-autonomous 'selves,' each of which is supported by certain relationships in the individual's life . . ." [7, p. 209]. "The Caring Paradox is that self-realization is only possible through caring for others. Caring for and about others *is* caring for ourselves. . . . We have impact on others by acknowledging their impact on us; we grow by supporting others' growth" [6, p. 24].

Love is expansive. When we create a value system that is meaningful, we wish to share the peace and fulfilment that comes with that meaning system. This is why religious foundations have been at the root of the development of hospitals, universities, colleges, and charities in North America, and throughout the world. However, meaning systems are not necessarily religious. Many persons, in coming to terms with their own sense of values, realize that all persons are in-relationship and are fulfilled in-relationship. We feel especially human when we give. "It is better to give than to receive" is not just a Christmas marketing ploy. It indicates a fundamental truth about what it is to be human. To love is to commit oneself to the well-being of the other. But to commit oneself to the other is also to receive the greatest gift that a human can receive.

SOCIAL SUPPORT

The Latin root of the word "support" implies "to carry from below." The meaning is clear when we refer to physical support as in "the desk supports my weight," or "the roof is supported by the beams in the ceiling." However, the idea of being carried from below is good analogically for psycho-social support. For most of our lives we are carried by others, individually or by the community or culture as a whole. "Care is a synonym for social support." Silverman tells us that care or social support entails feedback, continuity, and connection; that the support must be consciously given, in order to provide a movement from what was to what is yet to be, and the recognition that the person receiving the support is part of the community that is giving the support [8, p. 85].

Essentially, social support is the conscious affirmation of the person as s/he does whatever they need to do to learn new coping skills for their new life situation. As Dr. Jaco says in this volume, "social support can be viewed as providing an experience which validates the worth of the person and offers them a caring presence when they are troubled" [9, p. 9]. Whatever else it might be, as the authors in this volume attest, social support is being there with the person in need.

Social support must be consciously given and consciously received, that is, the person receiving the support must have the awareness that the person or community giving the support is doing so for the sake of giving support and not for some other sake [6, p. 50]. "We can mentally take the role of the person in distress, but is we don't have the corresponding empathetic feeling response. Helping isn't likely" [6, p. 15].

Social support requires empathy. As Carl Rogers states, empathy

> means entering the private perceptual world of the other and becoming thoroughly at home in it. It involves being sensitive, moment to moment, to the changing felt meanings which flow in this other person, to the fear or rage or tenderness or confusion or whatever, that he/she is experiencing. It means temporarily living in his/her life, moving about in it delicately without making judgements, sensing meanings of which he/she is scarcely aware, but not trying to uncover feelings of which the person is totally unaware, since this would be too threatening. It includes communicating your sensings of his/her world as you look with fresh and unfrightened eyes at elements of which the individual is fearful. It means frequently checking with him/her as to the accuracy of your sensings, and being guided by the responses you receive [Rogers, C. (1975), quoted in 6, p. 133].

Empathy means creating an atmosphere in which the person in distress is free to ask for what is needed. Speaking of children, Phyllis Silverman says "Our openness will affect the questions they ask, the kinds of answers they can accept, and the very nature of the dialogue. In creating this atmosphere we try to provide our children with tools that promote their ability to cope and adapt positively to the vicissitudes of life [2, pp. 234-235]. The benefit is not limited to children. Or rather, the benefit of empathy speaks to the child within all of us.

WHEN SOCIAL SUPPORT IS ABSENT

The research is fairly clear, grieving persons need others either in the informal support offered by family and friends, or in formal settings. "There was a significant positive relationship between the availability of social support and health: Individuals who had a great number of supportive relationships suffered from fewer depressive symptoms and somatic complaints than those with less social support but had similar effects on married and widowed individuals" [10, p. 222]. Dependency needs are so closely correlated with safety needs that individuals who lose the one on whom they depend are vulnerable to excessive anxiety and worry simply because they are deprived of the strong, reliable support they once had [11, p. 261].

CONCLUSION

In this chapter I have explored the philosophical roots of social support in the very nature of humanity. Persons are beings-in-relationship. As a result, we are most truly ourselves when we give and receive support. The other authors in this volume make the idea of social support more concrete and applicable to daily life.

REFERENCES

1. J. D. Morgan, The Knowledge of Death Is a Stimulus to Creativity, in *Meeting the Needs of Our Clients Creatively: The Impact of Art and Culture on Caregiving,* J. D. Morgan (ed.), Baywood, Amityville, New York, pp. 11-25, 2000.
2. P. R. Silverman, *Never Too Young to Know: Death in Children's Lives,* Oxford, New York, 2000.
3. T. Hobbes, *Leviathan,* H. W. Schneider (ed.), Bobbs Merrill, Indianapolis, 1958. (Original work published 1651.)
4. J. J. Rousseau, The Social Contract, in *Anthology of Right and Reason,* A. Fogothe (ed.), Mosby, St. Louis, pp. 291-297, 1972. (Original work published 1791.)
5. T. Aquinas, Summa theologiae I-II. q. 90, a. 2, in *Introduction to St. Thomas Aquinas,* A. Pegis (ed.), Modern Library, New York, pp. 609-616, 1948. (Original work published 1273.)
6. D. Larson, *The Helper's Journey: Working with People Facing Grief, Loss, and Life-Threatening Illness,* Research Press, Champaign, Illinois, 1993.
7. R. A. Neimeyer, N. J. Keesee, and B. V. Fortner, Loss and Meaning Reconstruction: Propositions and Procedures, in *Traumatic and Nontraumatic Loss and Bereavement: Clinical Theory and Practice,* R. Malkinson, S. S. Rubin, and E. Witztum (eds.), Psychological Press, Madison, Connecticut, 2000.
8. P. R. Silverman and S. L. Nickman, Children's Construction of Their Dead Parent, in *Continuing Bonds: A New Understanding of Grief,* D. Klass, P. R. Silverman, and S. Nickman (eds.), Taylor and Francis, Washington, D.C., 1996.

9. R. M. Jaco, Distinguishing Features of Social Support, Counseling, and Therapy, in *Social Support* (this volume), J. D. Morgan (ed.), Baywood, Amityville, New York, Chapter 2, 2001.
10. W. Stroebe and M. S. Stroebe, Determinants of Adjustment to Bereavement in Younger Widows and Widowers, in *Handbook of Bereavement: Theory, Research, and Intervention,* M. S. Stroebe, W. Stroebe, and R. O. Hansson (eds.), Cambridge University Press, Cambridge, 1999.
11. C. M. Sanders, Risk Factors in Bereavement, in *Handbook of Bereavement: Theory, Research, and Intervention,* M. S. Stroebe, W. Stroebe, and R. O. Hansson (eds.), Cambridge University Press, Cambridge, 1999.

CHAPTER 2

Distinguishing Features of Social Support, Counseling, and Therapy

Rose Marie Jaco

The purpose of this chapter is to distinguish among three components of helping often found in the field of grief counseling. These are social support, counseling, and therapy. Such distinctions can be useful because they allow helpers to select a technique that they deem will best meet the needs of their client at a particular time. In a very general sense, social support can be viewed as providing an experience which validates the worth of the person and offers them a caring presence when they are troubled. So necessary is social support to effective helping that this quality should always characterize both the helping environment and the helper's attitude toward the person in need. Social support can be seen as the essential backdrop against which all helping efforts are played out, including the provision of counseling and therapy. But there are also specific programs that helpers can provide that directly express social support to a client, and they will be examined below.

In general terms, counseling and therapy are specialized techniques that are used when the client requires professional help to deal with the emotions, changes, and choices they face as a result of a loss, life transition, or problem in living. This section of the book offers a review of social support, counseling, and therapy intended to define their nature so that they can be differentiated from each other, although the differences among them are not always clear and there is much overlap in their application. It will briefly examine methods of implementing each approach in bereavement work, and indicate circumstances when counseling or therapy is needed by a grieving person in addition to social support.

Social support is a concept that resembles other abstract ideas such as quality of life and happiness, in that its definition is elusive and its existence depends upon subjective experience. Nevertheless, attempts have been made to capture the essential nature of social support so that helpers in many fields can strengthen that aspect of their work, knowing that when social support is provided skillfully, great benefits can be realized by people in respect to their physical and psychological health. Social support has been defined as "verbal and non-verbal information, advice, tangible aid, or actions offered by others or drawn from their presence which has a beneficial and sustaining effect for the recipient" [1]. The core characteristic of social support is that it originates in interaction with other people, most frequently coming from the natural helping network of the person in need, which usually consists of family, friends, workmates, and neighbors. However, social networks outside the natural circle in which the person moves can be constructed through forming special purpose groups or gatherings where it is made easy for a person to encounter others in a similar situation and where it is possible to form supportive relationships based on common needs [2].

Although social support is a useful quality of daily life which enables people to deal more effectively with demands and frustrations, it is a resource which becomes an essential need for people who are experiencing an event in their lives which is felt deeply and which evokes strong emotions such as grief, abandonment, guilt, rejection, or shame. These feelings are often present in people grieving a death, and the response of the mourner's social system tends to be comforting and sustaining in response to the perceived need of the person. Yet this reaction may not always be present. Certain thinkers in the field believe that there is a two-way flow in the giving and receiving of social support. Although many people may connect supportively with those in need because of their warm and nurturing manner, and many recipients of support are open to receiving caring gestures and affirming words, there are others for whom the giving and receiving of support is problematic.

Some people may find it difficult to offer support to others, perhaps because of the element of emotional intensity which often accompanies the interaction and feelings of vulnerability they might experience when they offer their presence to someone who may come to depend on them. Others find it hard to seek and use support, based on earlier life experiences and prior relationships which have diminished their sense of trust. In addition, seeking help from another person may leave people with feelings of vulnerability and shame, based on cultural directives, particularly for men, which imply that adults should be able to manage stress independently without leaning on others. Some research indicates that people who perceive that they have social support are more likely to have attitudes which are strongly self-affirming, such as "a belief in one's interpersonal skills, feelings of self-efficacy leading to adaptive behavior under stress, low levels of anxiety, positive self-image, positive expectations about interaction with others, and a benign view of people" [2]. The idea that the offering of social support is mediated by the personality characteristics and attitudes of both the provider and the recipient offers a challenge for those who wish to create supportive interactions.

It means that they must prepare themselves carefully to communicate in an authentic, non-judgmental, sustaining manner, respecting the boundaries appropriate to the relationship while seeking ways of providing support to those in need that are as accessible and non-threatening as possible to many types of personality.

Helpers who wish to provide a high level of social support for their clients, and one that is most readily experienced by them as truly sustaining, have four elements to consider. These four are supportive environments, messages, interactions, and relationships. While the context of social support is found in relationship and interaction with others, communication is the means of conveying comforting messages to those in need. Communication begins with the *physical environment* in which interactions occur as it sends a strong message to those who enter that space. Ideally, the setting should be warm, welcoming, and appropriate for the clientele and the activities in which they are participating. Comfort and hospitality provide a supportive surrounding without words and facilitate connection with the client who is already reassured about their acceptance.

Supportive messages are characterized by empathy, which is the quality conveyed by the helper that they are able to enter, experience, and understand the client's world without being intrusive. The plight of the persons in need are acknowledged with warmth and understanding; they are encouraged to express their feelings and concerns and these are accepted as legitimate; their situation is given a context as part of the human condition, which serves to lessen social isolation; and instrumental help is given by providing information, appropriate advice, and by linking them to needed resources. *Interactions* are designed with the need of the client in mind, and may consist of face-to-face meetings or take place in a small support group or self-help group format. This may vary with the stage of grieving and must be decided on between helper and client. *Supportive relationships* result from helpers making themselves available to the person in need in an inviting, respectful, and accepting manner. It is easy for someone overwhelmed with a life event to experience a relationship which is intended to be supportive as manipulative, overwhelming, or insincere, particularly if their past encounters with significant people have been so. The helper needs to offer their presence with genuine concern, always respecting the person's need to establish their boundaries, make their own choices, and determine their own path.

Rando indicates that the mourner's perception of the nature of the social support available to them can be a positive or negative factor in their healing. "If the mourner perceives the world as providing support for mourning, that perception is an extremely positive factor. If the mourner perceives that support is unavailable, that it is available and not forthcoming, or that his loss is not socially acknowledged that perception can have a profound impact on coping and may constitute a high-risk factor for complicated mourning" [3, p. 495]. Certain aspects of providing and receiving social support are discussed by the author, including the fact that social support interactions are difficult to enact between two people who share grief about the same death. As well, "disenfranchised grief" related to a stigmatized death, the death of a person whom society devalues, or where a relationship existed which was not socially sanctioned, can result in the withholding of social support from the mourner, thereby intensifying his or her grief. In instances where the nature of the death or the relationship compromises the giving of support by natural helping networks, it is likely that the client would benefit from referral to a grief counselor or therapist.

Social support is often given in group format, sometimes by organizing mutual aid or self-help groups or through professionally led groups. Mutual aid groups consist of the joining together of people with similar experiences and needs, often under the guidance of a lay leader, to share feelings and coping strategies with one another. They can be most supportive and effective, with much depending on the presence in the group of people with healing capacities and on the skill of the leader. Professionally led groups tend to have clearer goals and processes, and can also be a source of real support for mourners. Support groups are intended to help members cope with distressing life events and enhance their coping and stress management skills. The group process for support groups has been described as follows. "The group worker helps members share their experiences and empathically respond to each other. Simply recounting events, ventilating feelings, and reflecting on efforts to cope can promote self-understanding and help overcome loneliness, isolation, and despair. The group worker also helps members overcome feelings of alienation, stigmatization, and isolation by validating, affirming, and normalizing their experiences" [4].

If social support must underlie all helping efforts in order to make them effective, we need to be able to determine the type of clients for whom social support alone is sufficient to enable them to do the work of grieving and those who require counseling or therapy. It is likely that when sufficient social support is provided by a mourner's natural helping network, and their grief is not complicated by depression or the extraordinary nature of the relationship or circumstances of the death, the person will not come to the attention of those working in the bereavement field. They will be able to complete the tasks of mourning within their natural life space, and in such a way that they are able to pick up the threads of their lives and move forward with creating a rewarding life. The formal provision of social support opportunities is needed for certain people, those whom Worden refers to doing less well with bereavement because they have "inadequate or conflicted social support" [5, p. 34] in their natural surround.

Worden suggests that "counseling or therapy may be required by other mourners where their grief is complicated by the traumatic circumstances of a death, a highly ambivalent relationship with the deceased, and the presence of concurrent life crises" [5, p. 41]. Rando considers mourners at greater risk for unresolved grief and its negative consequences when a death has been sudden, unexpected, caused by unnatural circumstances such as accident, suicide, or homicide, is multiple or traumatic in nature, or involves the loss of a child. She offers a helpful list of questions to enable an assessment to be made regarding a person's need for counseling or therapy, and should the answers indicate that the death was unexpected and the circumstances traumatic and that the person's life has been profoundly affected by the loss, referral for specialized help is indicated. The questions, slightly modified, are as follows [3, p. 249]:

1. What is the nature of the death and the circumstances surrounding it?
2. Was the loss expected or not, and how sudden was it?
3. What does the death mean to the mourner and how deeply will it affect his or her life?
4. What losses has the mourner experienced in the past and how have they coped with earlier losses?
5. What are the mourner's current life circumstances?
6. What forms of support are available from other people?

So difficult is it to accurately define counseling and therapy in ways that allow for distinctions to be made between the two activities, that many reference books have both terms in their title and are seen by some theorists as synonymous. However, attempts have been made to note the differences, and of these Shebib says: "Both counseling and psychotherapy strive to help clients to learn skills, deal with feelings, and manage problems. In counseling and psychotherapy, appropriate relationships with clients are the medium for promoting change. In both psychotherapy and counseling, these relationships with clients are crucial to success" [6, p. 3]. He goes on to say that the major difference between counseling and therapy is that therapy tends to be more long term because it emphasizes severe emotional and behavioral difficulties or disorders, whereas counseling is targeted toward assisting clients to manage problems-in-living. George and Christiani summarize the differences as follows: "counseling is more likely to emphasize activities that involve supportive, situational, problem-solving, conscious awareness, present-time and short-term concerns; and psychotherapy is more likely to emphasize activities that are reconstructive, depth emphasis, analytical, past-focussed and long-term" [7]. So closely allied are the disciplines that the same person may be trained to provide both counseling and therapy, and might often use the techniques associated with both disciplines in the same interview, and almost certainly in the same treatment program with a client, depending on the client's needs.

Counseling and therapy are professional activities for which people receive extensive education and training. Familiarity with a range of theories related to human development, relationships, emotional reactions, grief, and trauma provide guidelines for the professional to select interventions designed to strengthen the client to cope with the demands of their lives. In addition, professional helpers require skill training in how to conduct productive interviews and develop approaches that are sensitive to variations in client responses related to their personality, gender, age, culture, and values. The general focus of all counseling and therapy is to empower the client to use their personal strengths and natural networks in ways that enable them to cope with stress, loss, change, and growth. Worden recommends counseling to assist people in resolving what he refers to as "normal" or "uncomplicated grief," and this is designed to help the client work through an acute reaction to a death and to accomplish the four tasks all mourners must complete. These are: 1) to accept the reality of the loss; 2) to express all emotions connected to the deceased and their loss; 3) to resolve any problems related to the absence of the deceased in the mourner's life and to learn to live without their presence; and 4) to say a final good-bye and to begin to re-invest in life and in other relationships [5, p. 38 ff].

Worden goes on to note that sometimes a referral for therapy may be needed because the client is unable to use counseling to complete their work of mourning fully, and are in a state that he refers to as "complicated grief." At times, this involves a clinical depression and, although the symptoms of grieving and depression are similar, when feelings of sadness are enduring and pervasive, psychosocial functioning is severely compromised and physical symptoms of insomnia, fatigue, and appetite changes appear, the client needs a medical assessment to determine if depression is present. Complicated grief manifests itself in a variety of forms [5, chapters 4 and 5]. Because of aspects of the mourner's personality, circumstances of the death, an overload of personal losses, or absence of social support, people may react to the loss by developing chronic grief reactions, by exhibiting signs of post-traumatic stress disorder, by developing mental health problems, or by masking the grief with physical symptoms or maladaptive behavior. In these instances grief therapy is indicated with the specific goal of resolving the attachment issues that have been created or revived by the death. This work necessitates a careful examination of family of origin relationships and patterns, exploration of the personality traits of the client, expression and acceptance of the emotions attached to the deceased and the relationship, and the adoption of the client of a perspective that allows him or her to accept the reality of their situation and to move forward with their life freely and without guilt. Grief therapy may be long-term work, and requires the development of a trusting and supportive relationship between client and therapist.

Some general aspects of providing social support distinguish it from both counseling and therapy. Knowing that a supportive presence may be offered by many different people without specific training and often in an informal way distinguishes this form of helping from the professional activities of counseling and therapy. The major characteristics required of a supportive person are an attitude of respect, acceptance, and caring and the ability to engage with the person in need on a psychologically safe level, enabling them to share their feelings, needs, and thoughts openly. This is also true of the professional counselor or therapist, but in addition to this basic supportive stance the processional adds extensive knowledge of personality, relationships, crisis, and life transitions, as well as a set of therapeutic skills. Social support groups that come together for mutual sharing and encouragement also contrast with professional activities, which most frequently take place between counselor/therapist and client on a one-to-one basis, protected by strict rules regarding confidentiality. Both counseling and therapy can be offered in a group format, but in the professionally led group the structure and process are designed with theoretical principles as guidelines. The members must be carefully selected to promote the therapeutic impact of the group, and the group is managed according to the stages present in all groups and with reference to the dynamics of each group. In summary, social support is a quality that must be present in all inter-personal helping in order for the person in need to feel accepted, valued, and heard. For many bereaved people, social support is sufficient to enable them to do the work of mourning and move forward with their lives. Others will need either counseling or therapy, and perhaps a combination of both, in order to achieve healing from their grief. It is important for helpers in this field to distinguish among these three components of helping in order to provide clients with the most appropriate and helpful resource.

REFERENCES

1. B. W. Sheafor, C. R. Horejsi, and G. A. Horejsi, *Techniques and Guidelines for Social Work Practice,* Allyn & Bacon, Boston, 1997.
2. B. R. Burleson, T. L. Albrecht, and I. G. Sarason, *Communication of Social Support: Messages, Interactions, Relationships and Community,* Sage, Thousand Oaks, California, 1994.
3. T. A. Rando, *Treatment of Complicated Mourning,* Research Press, Champaign, Illinois, 1993.
4. R. W. Toseland and R. F. Rivas, *An Introduction to Group Work Practice,* Allyn & Bacon, Boston, 1998.
5. J. W. Worden, *Grief Counseling: A Handbook for the Mental Health Practitioner* (2nd Edition), Springer, New York, 1991.
6. B. Shebib, *Choices: Practical Interviewing and Counseling Skills,* Allyn & Bacon, Toronto, 2000.
7. R. L. George and T S. Christiani, *Counseling: Theory and Practice,* Allyn & Bacon, Toronto, 1995.

CHAPTER 3

Social Support for the Dying

Carol H. Ehrlich and Carolyn Jaffe

There are few events in the life of a human being that have the power to shake, upend, and totally transform his or her way of living, outlook and attitudes, planning and approach to everything thereafter. Those events may be more numerous for some individuals, but for everyone, they are birth and death. News of an expected birth and news of a death, impending or already experienced, will compel profound adjustments of an order never before experienced or appreciated.

A diagnosis of a life-threatening illness inevitably has a ton-of-bricks impact on the patient (and of course the family and friends as well), which will reside in the base of the patient's consciousness like an immutable weight from that moment on. Everything that happens, everything that is enjoyed, everything that is planned, every project executed, every interaction thereafter, with some possible brief reprieves of intense attention elsewhere, will be colored by knowing, down deep inside, "I am going to die."

How we human beings handle that knowledge varies as broadly as our population is wide. Many deny the diagnosis, as Kübler-Ross describes, some determinedly and to the end. Some deny at the start, then grow to respond in other ways. Many others rail to the last breath, as Dylan Thomas admonished in his well-known verse, "Do not go gentle into that good night, old age should burn and rave at close of day; rage, rage against the dying of the light." We can assume these persons have an overwhelming need to deny or to fight. Their defences require it.

And for others, for a variety of reasons, news of impending death may be or may be*come* a challenge—a challenge to find a way to cope with, even a way to find the good in dying . . . a challenge to experience dying in the best, most productive, satisfying way . . . a challenge to wind up one's life so loose ends are tied, so a good legacy is left. When the patient accepts this challenge he or she is accepting the dying.

All of these reactions, as different as they are, are legitimate. They are real. They are human. None of them is *wrong*. Understanding and respect are the only responses caregivers and professionals involved can make to these reactions, as we must give these patients the right to be themselves. By our words and by our actions, we can convey our appreciation of their needs and respect for their decisions. And whichever is their reaction, we can support them.

Social support for the dying must be viewed in an overall rubric of meeting the patients' needs. It is not isolated help of a psychological or spiritual nature. Social support for dying persons, to be effective, must encompass the whole person. The hospice movement has evolved to provide the broad and integrated support that is required. For the deny-ers and rail-ers, that support may be directed largely to the family, at least until acceptance becomes thinkable. For those patients already there, hospice has much to offer to the patient him- or herself.

The hospice movement is also beginning to offer a custom-tailored bridge support called palliative care which combines the best of hospice care with whatever active treatments the patient and physician may wish to continue, and is particularly helpful for the patient who has not fully accepted his dying. Palliative care is also becoming an option in some hospitals, and is in trial in some communities as a special program for children at any stage of a potentially life-limiting illness, whether in hospital or at home.

The essence of hospice is comfort care, as contrasted with a cure-driven plan of care. It supports the patient (and the patient's family) in a way that will provide for comfort throughout his or her dying. For that reason and because it is patient-centered, hospice is unique among health-care delivery systems. The voice that counts belongs to the patient, not to the physician or nurse, as in the medical model. The patient chooses his or her path for the days, weeks, or months of remaining life.

It is difficult to describe in a sentence or two the nature of the care and why it is so special.

The answer is bound up in two concepts. One is a holistic perspective, the other a dedicated, ongoing team. The two concepts are tightly interwoven. First the holistic perspective: The whole patient and his family are the focus, that is, the patient's physical being and his and his family's psychosocial selves and spiritual selves, not just the patient's body—or worse, body part. This comprehensive focus changes the nature of care entirely. The person and his significant others are affirmed as whole human beings of value for whom the care is given—and that becomes the foundation of social support.

Hospice care encompasses the patient's physical concerns: pain, infection, fatigue, sleeplessness, dizziness, nausea, inability to eat or swallow, shortness of breath and trouble breathing, stomach cramps, uncontrollable diarrhea, or any other distressing symptoms that can arise. It encompasses his capacity for activities of daily living, and the family's health around him. It takes in the patient's and family's psychosocial needs for support. It includes an awareness of and response to their yearning for an uplift of the spirit, for meaning from their lives and the dying they are experiencing. Hospice care is all of this. Furthermore, it is all of this in a unity, not in pieces.

Second, the team: The acceptance of the whole person in hospice care permeates all the members of a team. The team may include the nurse, an aide, and a volunteer. The physician (either the patient's own or the medical director if the patient is no longer being cared for by his or her own doctor), social worker, and chaplain are also on the team, either on-line or behind the scenes in staff conferences. Others are included as needed: nutritionist, therapist, psychologist, or psychiatrist. Each person plays a part, not in a narrow, role-defined way, but with an open and aware appreciation of the patient's and family's total needs and priorities. Professional boundaries are not important. Meeting needs is the primary goal of all. The initial orientation to this holistic approach together with frequent team meetings keeps hospice care tuned to human beings, not to the specific ailments of a disease.

Dame Cicely Saunders, who founded the modern hospice movement in London in 1967, made nursing the philosophical and theoretical basis for hospice care. She was educated first as a nurse, then added social work, medicine, and pharmacy to her vitae. She referred to herself as "a nurse with extras." Her hospice nursing model is contrasted with a medical model in the words *holistic* rather than *reductionistic, caring* instead of *curing, self- and team-care* instead of *physician-controlled care, symptom management* rather than *disease management, inclusion of family* rather than *focusing only on the patient,* and *maximizing quality of life* instead of *extending life.* Her philosophy continues to guide the expanding hospice movement today.

Continuity adds its magic to hospice's comfort care. Team members are the patient's own; once connected, they can identify with each other and build the trusting relationship necessary to produce comfort. Time is spent with the patient and his family, not just to carry out a task but with the purpose of meeting their needs. Teaching the member of the family or the friend who becomes the caregiver how to give a bed bath, for example, may be the nurse's responsibility; (s)he will spend the extra time needed to talk with the caregiver and patient about and respond to any worries or problems uncovered in the process. Threaded throughout these interactions is the nurse's example of an accepting view of death which helps to shape the caregiver's and patient's attitudes. Visits are open ended in order to permit this support. Reimbursement is structured to allow patient-oriented, not task-oriented care, with a per-diem rather than per-hour rate.

Clearly, this broader view of the role of the nurse, the aide, the physician, the social worker, the chaplain, and others who may participate in the team, requires that they be competent in human interactions and teaching as well as in their own professional arenas.

An integral part of this unique comfort care is building self-confidence in the patient and caregiver, for hospice aims to enable them to care for themselves and each other as much as possible. They are not consumers of health care being acted upon—thereby being put in a weak or infantilized role—but full participants in the team. By teaching the caregiver skills to make him or her feel competent and unafraid, hospice leaches much that is negative out of caring for someone who is dying. Fear is otherwise a paralyzing impediment to the caregiver's comfort as (s)he goes about the hard work of tending the patient. The point is that hospice is not a savior, but a friend and objective helper.

It is important, then, to consider what the patient and his family want and need from the hospice team. When asked, the answers have a common ring to them.

> I'd like a doctor (or team member—authors' comment) to scan *me,* to grope for my spirit as well as my prostate. Without such recognition, I am nothing but my illness [1].

> Be honest with me; listen to me. Give me hope. Let me be in control. Accept and support me. Know what you are doing. Don't encourage me to cry, but understand if I do. Don't give me routine reassurance. (Drawn from various patient comments.)

Successful care—care that will help the patient and his family and result in a positive experience at the end of life, must respond to these wishes.

EMPATHY

We consider empathy to be at the core of a good team member/patient relationship. Empathy is the projection of one's own personality into that of another, a sensing of what the other is experiencing. It has several components—emotional, moral, cognitive, communicative, and relational—which can but do not need to be analyzed in an intellectual way because we know empathy when we feel it. We distinguish it from sympathy and sentimentalism, neither of which is desirable.

Empathy, in its best sense, is a positive social quality. It is not manipulative; that is, an empathic response is not aimed at accomplishing some objective from the person responding. Empathy is pure; it happens because of the nature of the persons involved, like a gift. Empathy is simultaneously subjective and objective, close and distant, conscious in thought and intuitive in feeling. Patients and their families know they are heard and valued when they feel an empathic response.

Empathy doesn't just happen. It requires knowing the patient, both his typical pattern of response and him or her as a person. Knowing the patient, in turn, comes from listening, from caring enough to be willing to be involved, from participating in the relationship and the clinical context.

A commitment is negotiated in the course of building an empathic relationship. Typically and ideally, the patient asks questions to determine if the team member is a good person, a good professional, and whether that person will care about him. If satisfied, the patient makes overtures to him or her. On the other side, the team member looks at the patient to see if he has special needs, and whether their personalities might click. If that is positive, the hospice person may offer personal information to establish a common ground, and with a mutual lowering of the guard, may offer humor. And so the relationship builds. The process may be swift or take some time, and may occasionally be elusive, but when achieved, empathy in the relationship between patient and hospice worker adds crucial value to end-of-life care.

To the team member who feels it is not important that their "personalities click," and who regards his or her professional input as the only thing that really matters, we would urge another look. Certainly knowledge and expertise are crucial. But alone they are cold and abrupt. They become more effective and certainly provide more support if offered in a context of empathy.

The second author has known these trusting relationships with her patients; she knows the comfort and value of being able to express and receive honest feelings and thoughts. Patients with advanced disease have been able to ask their difficult questions, to let out their true worries and talk them through. She felt the patients' trust in order to answer their questions, sometimes with painful answers, perhaps with uncertain answers. Even when there can be no answer, this climate of trust and the necessary skills are important for an honest and helpful discussion. The core of the trust is telling the truth, which isn't always easy—but which hospice people become adept at doing.

Since not everyone is blessed equally with the capacity for empathy, it is important for the hospice team to let the members who are most effective in relating to the patient have the opportunity to allow these discussions to occur, for they are crucial to the support that is needed.

Relationships in the generic health care setting are of different types. They can be classified as clinical, therapeutic, connected, or over-involved. Our relationships in hospice aim at being connected. The hospice team regards the patient first as a person, like herself or himself—not as a "case"—in order to achieve a connected relationship. In that relationship, the team member can intercede for the patient, buffer him, and in general be his advocate, surely the best way to provide support. The patient in a connected relationship believes his advocate will go the extra mile, and he respects the advocate's judgment and feels grateful. The advocate believes his or her care makes a difference to the patient. The trust, the empathy, the reward to his spirit, all help the patient. The response, the connectedness, the success in helping, all reinforce the advocate. The relationship becomes one of the spirit, of their shared humanity. As in any warm, human relationship, both parties can feel reward and inspiration to go on.

The length of time in which the hospice person and patient can build this relationship will, of course, affect its quality. A patient's length of stay will depend on how early in his illness he is referred to hospice; what his functional status is; how much of his hospice time is spent in the hospital as opposed to actual hospice care; whether he is at home or in a free-standing or hospital hospice; whether caregiver support is available; and what comprises the team member's patient care mix.

(Rumblings within the hospice community and among enlightened physicians portend referrals being made earlier than the current few weeks or days before death.)

Because the dying patient is not an island, hospice care is directed to the family as well as the patients. Effective patient support demands this, because of the immediacy of their intimate relationships. What happens to the caregiver and family rubs off on the patient, and vice versa. Quality of life for the caregiver is enhanced by hospice support of his or her physical, emotional, social, and financial needs, and is directly affected by that caregiver's perception of the patient's quality of life. Hospice workers, patients, and caregivers become one unit in this end-of-life journey, and the care program recognizing that provides a uniquely effective service.

THE HOSPICE TEAM

The *primary care nurse* holds a large responsibility in hospice care. His or her skill and competence and human responsiveness will often set the tone of the hospice/patient and family relationship.

Selection of persons to be hospice nurses is done carefully in order to avoid problems of failure and burnout. Certain characteristics are necessary in addition to competence in the traditional nursing skills of managing complicated pumps, tricky medications, diet, bowel regularity, and skin care, to mention but a few. Special qualities include assertiveness and ability to operate productively without role restraints, to function under stress, and to make decisions and accept responsibility for them. Can this person work in a team? Deal with not being appreciated? Work with the pain of death? Balance his own life with his work, and avoid over-involvement and its handmaidens, rescuing and co-dependency?

Once engaged, nurses need support in order to give it. They find it helpful to have resources available to them that can undergird and recharge them. Hospice programs have arranged this with the provision of in-service meetings and formal retreats. Particularly when the staff of a hospice program grows large, annual retreats can be helpful to help workers rekindle passion and commitment, to discover ways to recover after a patient's death, and to consider their ideas in the forum of others' experiences. In addition, the availability of support personnel such as social workers and chaplains to nurses can mean help in their healing. These individuals can be a blessing when the days are hard.

Well-selected hospice nurses will have staying power if provided several other things: recognition, professional growth opportunities, the opportunity to participate in policy development, and occasional mental health days. Nurse managers who are strong leaders willing to discuss work problems with the staff facilitate job satisfaction among the nurses.

Clearly the attitudes and behaviors of nurses will affect the kind and amount of support they can provide the patients they serve. Leonard et al. have recommended certain attitudes and behaviors of nurses caring for the dying [2]. (They might well be extended to everyone on the hospice team.) They include:

1. Recognize the patient's and family's need for hope, control, accessibility, support, and normality.
2. Keep communications open.
3. Recognize and respect family characteristics, developmental stage, and coping mechanisms.
4. Avoid preconceived ideas of how families *should* cope.
5. Inform the family of resources available to them.
6. Allow the family to make use of these resources, and not be coerced into them.

These recommendations have power when team members truly manage to place themselves in the patient's position . . . experience what (s)he experiences, feel what (s)he feels. Periodic self-examination with the question, "How would I want to be treated?" leads to a determined effort to follow the recommendations, even when stress and overload make them easy to forget.

Skorupka and Bohnet went a step further. They studied caregivers' perceptions of nursing behaviors that were present in a home-care hospice setting, finding certain ones they regarded as most helpful and others least helpful out of a list of 75 behaviors [3]. The most helpful, as determined by all caregivers receiving service from this hospice, were:

1. Provide the patient with necessary emergency measures if the need arises.
2. Assure the patient that nursing service will be available 24 hours a day, 7 days a week.
3. Answer my (the caregiver's) questions honestly, openly, and willingly.
4. Allow the patient to do as much for himself as possible.
5. Teach me (the caregiver) how to keep the patient physically comfortable.

The behaviors held least helpful by all caregivers included:

1. Pray with me.
2. Plan for me to talk about my feelings with other people facing the same problems.
3. Help me to understand what the loss of the patient will mean to me.
4. Help me to make funeral arrangements.
5. Cry with me.

Sixty of those same behaviors were then ranked in another study within a different home-care hospice setting ten years later, finding a somewhat different set of caregivers' perceptions of the most and least helpful nursing behaviors [4]. That caregivers' list of most helpful nursing behaviors includes in descending order:

1. Listen to the patient and to what (s)he wants.
2. Provide the patient with the necessary emergency measures if the need arises.
3. Assure me that the nursing services will be available 24 hours a day, 7 days a week.
4. Answer the patient's questions honestly.
5. Talk to the patients to reduce their fears.
6. Provide me with information necessary if a home death occurs.
7. Answer my questions honestly, openly, and willingly.
8. Stay with the patient during difficult times.
9. Assure the patient that nursing services are available 24 hours a day, 7 days a week.
10. Teach me how to keep the patient physically comfortable.

The corresponding least helpful behaviors were:

1. Talk with me about my guilt.
2. Cry with me.
3. Help me to make funeral arrangements.
4. Attend the funeral when the patient dies.
5. Assist me in establishing a method for recording medications.
6. Teach me how to turn and position the patient.
7. Assist me in learning how to change the bed sheets with the patient in bed.
8. Recognize my need to talk about things unrelated to death.
9. Help me to face reality in my own way in my own time.
10. Assure me that the patient can be readmitted to the hospital if necessary.

In the more recent study, helpful behaviors most often addressed the patient's psychosocial need, then his physical needs, and last the caregiver's psychosocial needs. In contrast, at least from the available data, the most frequent category of need met by nursing behaviors in the early study was patient physical need, then caregiver psychosocial, and last patient psychosocial need.

This reversal may reveal a complex change in values, skills, and health care realities over the ten-year period between studies. Hospice had been communicating its purpose throughout this time so presumably there was a better understanding later of its holistic philosophy. Human relationship skills and the need to address patients' psychosocial needs had grown in importance while physical comfort had grown more achievable over these years, so perhaps it posed less of an unmet need.

Interestingly, the later study added the hospice nurses' view of their own most and least helpful behaviors in a home care hospice setting. They felt their most helpful behaviors were:

1. Assure the caregiver that nursing services will be available 24 hours a day, 7 days a week.
2. Teach the caregiver how to keep the patient physically comfortable.
3. Help the patient to feel safe ventilating anger, sadness, anxiety, and other feelings.
4. Answer the patient's questions honestly.
5. Listen to the patients and to their wants.
6. Assure the *patient* that nursing services are available 24 hours a day, 7 days a week.
7. Teach the caregiver how to relieve the patient's symptoms.
8. Provide the caregiver with the information necessary if a home death occurs.
9. Help the caregiver to feel safe ventilating anger, sadness, anxiety, and other feelings.
10. Recognize when the patient needs to talk about death and dying.

Hospice nurses regarded the least helpful nursing behaviors to be:

1. Describe how to keep the patient well groomed.
2. Assist the caregiver to provide a clean, neat environment for the patient.
3. Encourage the patient to have false hope.
4. Cry with the caregiver.
5. Pray with the caregiver.
6. Teach the caregiver to prevent long-term complications of bed rest.
7. Teach the caregiver how to adjust the diet as needed.

The nurses' list of helpful behaviors is similar to the caregivers', except they regard as more important establishing a climate in which caretakers and patients feel safe to vent their feelings. The authors agree strongly with the nurses in this study that establishing an accepting climate is crucial. It is the glue that keeps the various members of the effort together. It is the nutritional solution in the petrie dish that permits growth.

Another study, this one based on input from nurses and nurse educators, found "critical nursing behaviors," a somewhat different slice through the globe of nursing, comprised of responding during the actual dying, giving comfort, responding to anger, facilitating personal growth, working well with colleagues, supporting quality of life during dying, and being responsive to the family [5].

Defining the most and least helpful things hospice nurses do is useful to programs providing their training, useful to nurses on the job, and useful to hospice administrators who must evaluate staff performance. It is helpful, ultimately, to the dying patients and their families, for it enhances the capacity of hospice to provide support.

Some nursing care can be handled by persons less-trained than registered nurses. *Certified Nurse Aides* carry out important parts of the job, providing further competent coverage at lower cost. CNAs have certain requirements and qualifications, such as having current certification and a valid driver's license with liability insurance (or the ability to get to the patient's home via public transportation), completing hospice training and attending all in-service training sessions, and acquiring some defined number of Continuing Education Credits each year. They participate in team meetings. Following planning with the staffing coordinator and the primary care nurse, CNAs are responsible for providing many personal care services, according to federal and state regulations. They keep timely records of their care and provide miscellaneous support to the patient and family. They give no medications, and commonly provide no supervision.

Home Health Aides and *volunteers* comprise other unique aspects of the hospice experience, and are considered by many to be invaluable braces supporting the hospice tree without which the branches would break. Now numbering more than 90,000 in the United States, volunteers provide an enormous service as integral members of the hospice teams. Their service enriches the comfort care provided to patients and their families, and reduces the cost of this form of health care. Volunteers may assist with household and personal tasks, fitting into the dynamics of each situation. They can be the link between professional staff and members of the family, helping with their practical needs and providing emotional support. In communities across the country, the dying patients and their families often regard volunteers as their most personal and sometimes meaningful support.

Hospice home health aides and volunteers, men and women, are well trained. They must attend educational programs and be certified before beginning their work. Their training orients them in some depth to the hospice philosophy and principles, and to what will be expected of them. The teaching aims to blend fact, methodology, creativity, and personal style in a way the volunteers can utilize so they can function under various and dynamic circumstances. The training is not a drill to teach and improve task performance. It is geared to inform and inspire, and to stimulate personal growth so the aide and volunteer can step in with a grasp sufficient to respond to the wide variety of needs with which they will be faced.

The National Home Caring Council of the Foundation for Hospice and Homecare in 1990 developed a "Model Curriculum and Teaching Guide for the Instruction of the Homemaker-Home Health Aide (with the help of the Administration on Aging in the federal Department of Health and Human Services), which has provided guidance to local hospice organizations in planning their home health aide and volunteer training programs. Various hospice organizations and associations have added their ideas to this curriculum since then.

A typical curriculum aimed at certification of volunteers includes roughly thirty hours of didactic and seminar training, which must be completed before field training can begin. Lectures cover the history and philosophy of hospice, the mechanics of its operation, the holistic approach to pain control, interpersonal and family dynamics, team functioning, AIDS care, medical options when palliative care is part of the program, and presentations of personal stories. Training exercises generally include experience with team building and values determination. Short movies demonstrating home and in-patient care and an opportunity for participants to know each other may round out an intensive schooling from which volunteers can move with some confidence into their field training with staff members, and ultimately into their work. Even after all of that, volunteers are encouraged to attend in-service education and other programs.

Volunteers must have human qualities of warmth and caring, along with "people skills," and they need to be able to tolerate pain and suffering. Often the training program serves as a screening process: well-meaning students may realize as they learn about hospice that they are not cut out to be hospice volunteers. Those who proceed, by and large, become productive and successful volunteers.

At times, further screening has been regarded as necessary because, in spite of everything, a few volunteers do not work out satisfactorily. They may not have completed their own grieving over loss; they may not find the commitment workable in their lives; they may have had inappropriate reasons for volunteering.

An effort has been made to screen prospective volunteers using a psychiatrist-designed list of motivations for seeking such work. Applicants whose motivations were felt to be congruent with hospice work were accepted for the training program [6]. How much this is used, and how valid a tool it has been, is unknown to the authors.

The support provided by volunteers may differ in a qualitative way between the sexes. While all of the volunteers had sensing and judging traits, men in a recent study tended to be introverted and thinking. The women were often extroverted and feeling personality types. Being aware that these gender differences may exist can be helpful in recruitment, training, placement, and retention of hospice volunteers.

When all works out and the volunteers are actively participating in their teams, they need feedback about their work. Without a good sense of how they are doing they can feel unsure of themselves, become hesitant, and ultimately turn away from the work they had initially adopted with enthusiasm.

Most helpful is honest and direct informal feedback from the volunteer coordinator and the primary nurse with whom the volunteer works. A formal tool was devised, similar to a job performance evaluation in the commercial or industrial workplace, to enhance the assessment and provide tools for the volunteers' growth. Coordinators of volunteers from around the country developed criteria for satisfactory performance that were ranked in importance and grouped into four categories. The resulting performance checklist follows [7].

Commitment to the Program

1. Takes on cases when s/he is needed, according to agreement made with volunteer coordinator.

2. Works the number of hours per week agreed to with patient, family, or coordinator.

3. Makes home visits on the days and at the times expected by the patient or family.

Relationship to Patients and Family

4. Demonstrates the ability to be a good listener.
5. Does not preach or push his/her own religious ideas or practices.
6. Extends warmth and caring to patients and their families.
7. Behaves in a relaxed and calm manner around patients and families.
8. Sees the needs of patients and families and responds well to them.
9. Demonstrates the ability to remain engaged with the patient despite the physical or mental deterioration of that patient.
10. Does not try to take charge and get the family to do things his or her way.
11. Responds flexibly to changes in patient or family status.
12. Demonstrates the ability to cope with very stressful family situations.
13. Does not burden the patient or family with her/his personal problems or previous losses.

Team Member Functions

14. Demonstrates an acceptance of hospice philosophy and policies.
15. Reports any significant changes to the team immediately.
16. Complies reliably with required documentation.
17. Reports honestly and openly about cases to the volunteer coordinator.
18. Keeps hospice business confidential.
19. Keeps in touch with the volunteer coordinator or other designated team member to share and receive case information.
20. Consults with team members before making any changes in patient or family care.
21. Informs the volunteer coordinator, patient, or family when s/he cannot keep a scheduled appointment, in sufficient time so that alternate arrangements can be made.
22. Demonstrates the ability to accept supervision and to learn from it.
23. Demonstrates the ability to accept support from and give support to team members.

Self Awareness

24. Does not get overly involved emotionally with patients or their families.
25. Knows when s/he needs a rest and tells volunteer coordinator.

26. Maintains professionally appropriate appearance and hygiene.
27. Able to say "no" when s/he knows that at some level s/he would resent saying "yes" to the patient, family, or the volunteer coordinator.

This checklist, or a variation thereof, is used by many hospice organizations today.

Once found, a good volunteer must be nurtured in order to maintain his or her motivation. It helps if the volunteer's expectations in the work are met. Additionally, he or she must be made to feel like a valued team member. The feedback described above should confirm that. Growth of a hospice program from a small, family-feeling operation to a larger, more diverse and geographically dispersed organization makes this sense of intimacy and belonging more difficult to maintain, so efforts should be strengthened when the program grows.

Maintaining a strong volunteer side of the program is essential. It can spell success or failure for a hospice organization.

Hospice social workers are traditionally the ones thought of as the source of social support to the dying. They are, indeed, important members of the team and, in the authors' paradigm, equal to the other team members in their contribution to the support the patient feels.

Social workers are flexible in their roles. Some hospice programs are directed by social workers. In some programs social workers lead team meetings. Most often, social workers are on-line members of the team, providing support and services within the logistics plan of the particular hospice program. For example, social workers (often called family counselors) sometimes are scheduled to respond following the nurse's initial visit to a family—routinely when there are children, and upon request of the patient when there are not. In some programs they may be the first person to see the patient and family. Whether they provide the first or later contact with the patient and family, their beginning role is to explore with them their circumstances and feelings about admission to hospice in the *intake interview.* From their first conversation, the family counselors gain insights about the family's strengths, potential problems, and resources that are added to the initial assessment for the team who will be working with the family. Then the social workers participate in the ongoing planning that takes place in team meetings held during the service for any patient. They may see the patient and/or family members to provide support as time goes by. They are on call during off hours, just as nurses are, for emergencies such as interpersonal crises, threats of suicide, etc. Social workers provide information and help with arrangements regarding insurance, contacting persons or agencies when needed.

Typically social workers and chaplains plan and put on memorial services, held one or more times a year for both recently and more distantly bereaved families, at which the attendees are invited to share their memories.

Social workers may also provide support for nurses, aides, volunteers, and other team members under stress. Both patient and staff reap the benefits of having a social worker on the team.

The hospice chaplain also serves both the patient/family and the staff. Some of the most important issues faced by all persons trying to adjust to end-of-life realities are matters of the spirit. Many persons in this situation have within their own beings or circle of intimates the resources to resolve and deal with these matters, but some may be troubled and wish for help. When care is needed, they may call on their own clergyperson or the hospice chaplain. Hospice programs generally have a chaplain on staff or available to them when these needs arise. The chaplains' help to patients, families, and to team members is often vital and invaluable.

Because comfort care can require attention to physical complaints—pain, infection, problems with eating, sleeping, or breathing, or disability of some sort—*the physician* must be part of the team. No one else is equipped or authorized to prescribe medication for these problems. Most often the patient's own doctor continues to provide the service needed, and the valued doctor/patient relationship continues in the new context of the team. But we have occasionally been involved with patients who had no physician. They may have moved to be near a child or parent, or their physicians may have been reluctant to refer them for hospice care, so they chose to come independently, leaving their physicians. In these cases the medical director of the hospice program will assume responsibility, an essential part of the total hospice care.

The growth of the concept of palliative care, with its potential for integrated active treatment, has increased the role of the physician in some programs, particularly in hospitals. Where the time constraints of busy physicians allow, this expanded role may involve him or her more directly in the course of the patient's dying, even moving that essentially clinical relationship toward a connected one, thus contributing to social support for the dying patient.

The ease with which the nurse, the aide, the social worker, the chaplain, the physician, the volunteer, or any other member of the hospice team, can be called on to enrich a patient's care is part of what makes the hospice experience very different from other delivery systems. No roadblocks interfere with their participation and service; not financial, as reimbursement is based on an overall per-diem rate; not organizational, as service is structured in the context of the team.

Combine the assets of the team with hospice's holistic approach to comfort care, and you have a special gift to the dying and their loved ones, indeed. The hope is always to help them draw some value from the time that remains, and to enable them to reach some acceptance and peace in the end. Hospice is an option now available in most parts of the United States, one that offers care that provides true social support for the dying.

IT IS TIME

Our wholeness stands luminous
against life's curtain of noise . . .
No more of transient changes,
of trappings taken on, of conflicts.
No more dressing
in raiment not our own.

With each goodbye, each flower's embrace,
each easing of pain, each love expressed,
we strip away and—like a single red rose
or a Puccini aria in a now-empty hall—
become essence, ourselves,
whole and ready
at peace in the moment
for whatever lies ahead.

Carol H. Ehrlich

REFERENCES

1. A. Broyard, *Intoxicated by My Illness,* Clarkson N. Potter, New York, 1992.
2. Included by permission of *Cancer Nursing.* From Prolonged Cancer Death: A Family Affair, in *Cancer Nursing, 18*:3, pp. 222-227, 1995.
3. Included by permission of *Cancer Nursing.* From Primary Caregivers' Perceptions of Nursing Behaviors that Best Meet the Needs in a Home Care Hospice Setting, *Cancer Nursing, 5*:5, pp. 371-374, 1982.
4. P. Y. Ryan, Perceptions of the Most Helpful Nursing Behaviors in a Home-Care Hospice Setting: Caregivers and Nurses, *The American Journal of Palliative Care, 9*:5, pp. 23-29, 1992.
5. L. F. Degner, C. M. Gow, and L. A. Thompson, Critical Nursing Behaviors in Care for the Dying, *Cancer Nursing, 14*:5, pp. 246-253, 1991.
6. H. M. Houston, Screening Hospice Volunteers: Using a Psychiatric Nurse as a Consultant, *Hospital Topics, 59*:6, pp. 33-36, 1981.
7. B. Lafer and S. Craig, The Evaluation of Hospice Home Care Volunteers, *The Hospice Journal, 9*:1, pp. 13-20, 1993.

CHAPTER 4

Social Support of the Bereaved: Some Practical Suggestions

Darcy Nichols

When I was asked to write a chapter on social support for the bereaved, I was delighted but a little daunted by the task. There is a lot of literature that has been written on this topic by many well-known researchers in the field of bereavement study, and I felt that I probably have little to add to this research. However, in my role as a bereavement counselor, I do work daily with individuals who are grieving and I thought that sharing insights from "being in the trenches" might add a more personal side to what is already known through the research. So, I am presenting a more "hands on" discussion about social support for the bereaved—the things that strike me as helpful or not helpful and feedback I've received from some of my clients and friends regarding support that has been offered during a time of grief.

Those of us who have studied theories of bereavement are well aware of the importance of social support and its role in the "working through" of the grieving process. We teach this concept to our students, offer it as permission to our clients, and try to act on it with our grieving friends. We even "prescribe our own medicine" when we are grieving and know that we somehow need to reach out to others for our own support when we are hurting. But what exactly does it mean to offer social support? What are the details involved in offering social support to grieving individuals? Is it as simple as a phone call or a visit, or is it a more complex matter than that? I'd like to use this chapter to explore some of these questions and the issues they raise.

The first place I will start is to look at the dynamic of social support itself. We often assume that as long as there are people around the grieving person, all should be well and the normal grieving process will unfold. However, in reality, social support seems more like a two-way street, where it is important that social support be both available to *and* received by the grieving individual. There may be many people willing to offer support to the grieving individual, but perhaps there are factors that prevent the individual from being able to accept what is being offered. I think it would be safe to assume that there are internal factors to consider (aspects pertaining to the bereaved individual) and then there are external factors (aspects that reside out of the bereaved person's inner world), both of which mediate the role of social support in any one person. Each of these factors will be explored in order to have a better understanding of what it means to offer support sensitively and develop realistic expectations regarding the needs of the individual.

Logistical considerations may also be important. These considerations may seem obvious, but in asking them we are performing a self-check, trying to avoid imposing our values and ideas upon a person who has values and ideas that are unique and may differ from ours. For example, who does the bereaved individual *want* for support? Where is the best place for it to be offered? When is the best time or what is the best timing? How is the support that is offered being perceived by the grieving person? Answers to these questions do not reside within us, but within the person to whom we are offering assistance. We also cannot assume that we know what is best for another person by projecting onto that person what we would want, need, or feel if we were in his or her situation, although this projection may be an important precursor to an empathetic relationship being established.

FACTORS PERTAINING TO THE GRIEVING INDIVIDUAL

When a client walks into my office the first time, I try to find out what his or her expectations are from me and what this person perceives to be his or her needs. Usually, I tend to be direct and ask the person these things outright. As a griever, I have found when someone has attempted to reach out to me, it has been most helpful when they simply ask, "What do you need right now?" or "Is there something specific that you would like from me?" Of course, most grieving individuals would tell you that what they need is for the lost person(s) to return and come back into their lives, and anything else is secondary to that need. However, after that initial reaction, being asked to describe one's own needs is much more empowering than an outsider presuming to know what an individual's needs are, and taking the time to ask tells the person you want to be sensitive to him or her. In addition, taking time to think about one's needs and permission to explore feeling "needy" in a positive way can be very healing.

I often hear people tell me that they are angry with the individuals who tend to tell them what they should be feeling or doing instead of hearing from the bereaved individual what his or her experience actually is. Comments like, "You should be moving on with your life now," or "You're holding up so well," and

"You should/shouldn't feel that way" may come from well-meaning individuals, but are often felt as external pressure to conform to expectations. What I am describing is different from normalizing the grieving process, where a helper reflects on the griever's experiences in light of what is known about grief. Allowing the grieving individual the safety to explore feelings, experiences, and perceptions without fear of judgment or the imposition of an agenda is probably the first step in offering social support.

Grief is defined as an individual's unique response to a loss. Even though the experience of grief is universal to all humans, each response to loss is both individual and unique—each of us grieves differently [1, p. 9]. Only the individual griever knows what is best and only she or he can truly define what social support is in light of her or his needs. Thus, my definition of social support centers completely on the perceptions and needs of the bereaved individual. Social support is the availability of a caring person to offer *what* the bereaved individual needs in the *way* that the bereaved individual chooses to receive it *when* the bereaved individual *wants* it. Social support is *whatever the grieving individual perceives it to be and needs it to be at any given time.* Effective social support would entail sensitivity to the pragmatic questions described earlier (who, what, where, when), and a willingness to offer support within the definition of what is supportive to the individual receiving it.

FACTORS INTERNAL TO THE INDIVIDUAL

Temperament and personality are important variables in this process. I am interested in these traits not just because I tend to be psychologically minded. In my training in counseling, the importance of the actual relationship between the client and the helper was emphasized as the most important therapeutic tool over any form of intervention strategy, theoretical foundation, or knowledge base. If the relationship itself is so important, then it would behoove those of us who are offering support to understand basic diversity in personality and temperament so we are aware of issues that might arise as a result of the dynamics created by these traits in the relational context.

I basically look for a few common personality traits/preferences as I am interacting with clients. I think about whether this person is more introverted or extroverted. An introvert may prefer to share with one person at a time and may only want to share his or her grief with one or two individuals. Introverts may also need time alone to process what has happened, and may tend to avoid groups (especially when feeling emotionally vulnerable). An extrovert may have a higher need to be around others in the grieving process and may have more of a desire to do grief work in the presence of others. Extroverts may readily gravitate toward bereavement groups for additional support and may feel being alone increases the pain of their grief.[1] In terms of the relational dynamics in a therapeutic setting, an introverted helper might tend to feel flooded by a highly extroverted client or an extroverted helper may overwhelm an introverted client. In working with an introverted person, I would be aware that group work may seem intrusive (especially early in the grief process), that "down time" would probably be very important, and that an introverted individual may feel overwhelmed by many people offering support all at once. For extroverted clients, I would try to find group activities that are available and recognize that extroverted individuals may need to be busy and active as part of their grief process. Thinking about these differences helps me to be sensitive to the client's preferences over my own and also to be aware of my own needs in working with diverse clients.

Another personality preference that I explore is if the person tends to experience their world more through emotions or through cognitive processes (sometimes called the "heart versus the head" dichotomy). Does this person tend to use the language of "I feel" more than "I think" or vice-versa? Exploring this trait helps me to respect a person's "language" of how she or he "takes in" the world. Someone who functions more from their "gut" may desire to deeply explore intense emotions and may use my support as a catharsis for expression and may want help in finding ways to experience these emotions in healthy ways. Individuals who function more from their emotions may have more difficulty dealing with the pragmatic aspects of a loss—paperwork, financial arrangements, and logistical considerations.

Individuals who tend to be more analytical in their worldview may be more distressed by things not "making sense" and need to ponder these issues as part of their grieving process. Their grief may be manifesting itself through cognitive disruptions more than emotional triggers. Individuals who are analytical in their processing may have difficulty dealing with emotions if they are coming to the surface and may need help in articulating their feelings, as it might seem like speaking a foreign language. Certainly, the challenges between a helper and client here would be obvious as well. I tend to be more of a feeling-oriented person. This works well for most of my clients, and I find I am comfortable in the language of emotions and their expression. However, it is sometimes a stretch for me to work with analytically-oriented clients, as their emotions are not often the main focus of their grief response. In these situations, I have to be careful not to impose what my own grief response would be onto someone else whose response is different than mine.

As I write these words, I think of lectures I have attended and literature I have read that seem to imply that all grieving individuals need to express their feelings openly in order to heal. It would seem that to some, the goal of bereavement counseling is to get bereaved individuals to emote. However, I wonder if we

[1] For more information on personality traits discussed in this chapter, see [2, 3].

devalue an individual's unique expression of grief when we assume that she or he is not grieving in a healthy manner unless emotions are being expressed outwardly and with intensity. It is also important to consider aspects of personal control and helplessness, which are significant after the loss of a loved one. Intense emotions can be overwhelming and may increase the sense of loss of control and powerlessness that the bereaved individual is already experiencing. We do well to tread lightly in this area while at the same time allowing the emotions of grief to be expressed and channeled as they do arise.

Elaine Aron [4] has conducted research on a temperament trait in certain individuals she calls "highly sensitive." Individuals who are highly sensitive tend to be easily flooded by external stimuli, such as noises, smells, being exposed to violent movies or TV shows, loud music, and to life event changes. These individuals often experience their emotions and thoughts very deeply and intensely as well. Aron describes these individuals as frequently labeled in Western culture as "weak," "overly emotional," "feminine," and "too intense." As a result, most highly sensitive individuals have already experienced a significant amount of social stigma and misunderstanding as they have gone through their life experiences.

For any individual, experiencing raw grief can feel stigmatizing—others do not know how to respond to the intense emotions of grief and may tend to avoid proximity to grieving individuals due to their own discomfort. Grieving individuals frequently report feeling embarrassed when they are emotionally triggered when they are in public places. For highly sensitive individuals who are already familiar with the feelings of shame from being labeled as "overly emotional" or "too intense," being absorbed into the grieving process simply adds insult to injury. In these individuals, trust can be difficult to establish because of repetitive experiences of rejection, misunderstanding, or alienation from past experiences. If I sense that there has been a history of repeated stigma surrounding emotions and life experiences, I may explore the topic of sensitivity and the client's experiences from the past as a way of giving permission for the intensity that may be present in an individual's grieving process. Some of the clients with whom I work have read information regarding the trait of sensitivity and found the descriptions and awareness of their own sensitivity to be useful in understanding and normalizing their reactions in the grieving process, therefore giving themselves greater freedom to grieve in their own unique way.

FACTORS EXTERNAL TO THE INDIVIDUAL

Certainly, there are many "external" forces that shape an individual's response to the offer of social support. The role of socialization in the individual's life through various influences is important to consider. Gender roles and socialization commonly mediate receptivity to offers of support. Although not consistently "black and white," in Western culture men tend to be socialized toward independence, stoicism, and a hierarchical way of relating to others [5, pp. 340-343]. A gesture of support from someone may be interpreted as identifying a weakness in the grieving man unless it is offered in a way that is congruent with male patterns of socialization. Offering to get together to "do something" may be more acceptable than offering to get together to "talk." I have found it interesting in my clinical practice to find that many male grievers prefer a female counselor because they feel more able to talk about issues that are tied to vulnerability and emotions with a woman. Choice of language may also be important. Rather than asking a grieving man to describe his feelings, I may ask for him to tell me what it's been like to lose someone, and I may avoid using the word "feelings" unless he uses the word first.

Professional socialization may also play a large role in how a grieving individual views the role of social support. In the workplace, people often compartmentalize their personal feelings and experiences in order to fulfill their professional roles. In our society, most grieving individuals are given minimal time away from work in order to "take care of business" when a death occurs. Returning to work after a brief funeral leave means these individuals are often still in shock or are numb when they attempt to resume their work duties. However, when the grieving process begins to surface emotionally, cognitively, physically, and/or socially, there is often little room to ask for support in an environment focused on productivity and "professionalism" defined by control over one's emotions. Furthermore, the possibility of losing income or being seen as "unable to perform" can present further threats to the grieving individual in addition to the stress of the loss of someone significant.

Coworkers may offer support and condolences, but their offers may present a mixed package. Does the bereaved individual risk disclosing the depth of impairment he or she is experiencing with someone in an environment that is often competitive and hierarchical? If the grief is not acknowledged openly, a lot of emotional energy might be expended trying to stay "in control" and present outward appearances of being "fine" when the inward reality is very different. Thus, accepting support in this environment may be very difficult, even if it is offered.

Messages taught within family units certainly affect how social support can be offered and how it may be received. Have the individual members of the family been taught to "keep things in the family" or not to "air out dirty laundry in public"? What have been the messages in the family about expressing emotions or discussing painful issues? In addition, the dynamics of interactions between family members are usually intensified after a loss. In most families, there is variation in the type of relationship each individual member shared with the deceased person and also in the ways each member experiences grief. Even though the members are grieving the same person, they often lack the ability to support each other because of these differences. Personality conflicts and dynamics between the members, old unfinished business, and family rules that do not allow for open expressions of thoughts or feelings may prevent the members from supporting each other or from accepting support offered from someone outside the family unit.

As I reflect on my own practice and experiences with families, I think of how often I receive phone calls from one family member asking for me to "help" another member. I think this request highlights how often family members are unable to be direct or open with each other regarding intense feelings or difficult events. Working with grieving families or couples as a unit is very different from working with individuals. In working with a family unit that is under stress, I try at first to align myself with the dynamics of the family rather than trying to move them into what I might perceive to be a more "healthy" pattern, unless I have concerns about the physical or emotional safety of one of the members. A time of crisis is not the optimal time to try to restructure old family patterns, and most families will rely on what is familiar to guide interactions even if these same patterns seem dysfunctional to an outsider.

Religious beliefs and spirituality may also affect how an individual receives support that is offered. Often, a person's religious practices dictate what is "appropriate" grief in terms of what emotions are acceptable, what activities are seen as appropriate, and who is reasonable to offer that support. Many individuals ask me about my own religious beliefs when calling to make an appointment for counseling, and I recognize that it is an important issue for them. I may have the best intentions when I offer my support to a grieving individual, but my support may go unrecognized if I am unable to share their belief system. In addition, people who are members of the clergy or religious authority figures cannot be separated from their professions easily by others. If a grieving individual is struggling with issues around faith, meaning, ambivalence, or anger toward God, support that is offered from a religious leader or representative may not be received because of what the helper represents, even if the intentions of the helper are to honor the grieving person's process.

Another factor I have become aware of is what I call the concept of "support overload." This concept has to do mostly with the question of timing. When a loss first occurs, the bereaved individual is often flooded with people offering many things—condolences, food, phone calls, cards, and letters with special thoughts or remembrances.

I actually had a client tell me that she left her house during the wake after the funeral and went for a walk because she could not handle so many people approaching her all at once and wanting her to talk about things that were so difficult (she was probably an introvert!). Most of us are aware that when a loss first occurs, most grieving individuals are in shock and unable to "take in" all that is offered. Many of the clients I work with have told me they didn't open sympathy cards for several months after the death occurred because it felt like "too much" to handle at the time. Others have told me that their need for support came at a time when most of the individuals in their support system assumed it was time to "move on" in life. Many widows have mentioned they didn't start to feel their emotions for a year after the death of their husbands. I hear stories about how difficult the second Christmas was because the person is no longer numb or in shock.

When I am asked to give public presentations on grief to people who want to effectively reach out to bereaved individuals, I suggest that they make a notation on their calendars as to the day a person died, and mark the specific times throughout the next year that they will be in touch with the grieving person. I try to educate about the importance of anniversary dates and holidays—times that are often not recognized for their significance to grieving individuals. If there are many others doing the same, the grieving individual may choose only one or two people with whom to share deeply. However, it is a good thing that the bereaved person has choices about what to share with whom rather than feeling isolated and alone in the grief journey. If I know a bereaved person has many people around him or her, I don't make the assumption that support needs are being met without offering my own support first. I am also aware that I cannot separate my identity from being seen as a "grief professional" to many people, and there will be associations with my work that may either encourage or discourage someone from allowing me to be a part of the grieving process.

THOUGHTS FOR THOSE OFFERING SUPPORT

In offering support to someone who is grieving, I try to keep some things in my own conscious awareness. The first thing I consider when I am offering support is to think about what I can realistically offer to someone. I try to remember that I do have limitations physically and emotionally. I think about the other demands that are being placed upon me at the time I want to offer help to someone and I evaluate these other demands in order to try to be realistic with my offer. I also keep this in mind when I am tempted to add another client to my schedule when I know my schedule is already full. My purpose in doing this isn't to prevent myself from reaching out to others. Rather, it is a way that I can reach out to others and be concrete, sincere, and realistic. That way, I do not feel that I have offered something that I cannot possibly maintain, which might feel like abandonment to the person who is grieving and prevent me from trying to maintain some form of ongoing contact because I feel guilty for not following through with more. Often, I am very specific with an individual about what I can offer and I try to state this directly. I also realize that I have to set priorities in order to be able to stay true to myself. My family must come first. My body needs rest, exercise, and good nutrition. I know that, emotionally, I need time to "digest" intense experiences, and working with grieving individuals can be very intense. All of these factors help me to make realistic choices in the ways that I can offer support.

I once read that saying "yes" means nothing if you are unable to say "no." This made a lot of sense to me. Thus, when I am offering support, I want to be able to "mean it," and I am honest with myself and with others about my limitations. If I take care of myself, then I won't engage the grieving person in a process of trying to look out for my needs in addition to his or her own. I think helping professionals often struggle with this issue, and the feelings that result can be very difficult to sort through.

Although each of us would like to take the pain away from the person who is hurting deeply, realizing that we cannot "make it all better" is the first step in offering the gift of presence to a grieving individual. We cannot bring back the person who died. We cannot take away the pain of grief. Our desire to offer support does not include trying to rescue from pain; instead, it is an offer to journey with someone who is in pain so he or she won't have to go through the pain alone. Over the years, my motto has become that I can't make it better but I will try to make a difference.

PRAGMATIC SUGGESTIONS

I am often asked, "What should I say to someone who has lost a loved one"? Many people tell me they do not contact bereaved individuals that they know because they either don't know what to say or they are afraid they will say the wrong thing. Many bereaved individuals tell me that they feel isolated and can sense the discomfort of others around them.[2] So, how can we bridge this gap? It is important to keep in mind that we live in a culture that values productivity, activity, and "doing." We do not feel we have given anything of significance to a grieving individual unless we have "done" something for them. However, the greatest gift we can offer to someone in pain or turmoil is simply our presence. Instead of "doing," we are "being." Sometimes, this is called the "gift of presence." Allowing silence, simply being with the grieving person quietly, providing companionship—all are examples of this gift. Its importance cannot be overestimated, yet our society tends to devalue it because there is no concrete "outcome" that can be measured as a result of its offering. I often make the statement, "Don't just do something—sit there!" It can be very hard to get comfortable with this idea when we have been indoctrinated with the value of "busy-ness."

I hear frequently from bereaved individuals that it is very hard to identify specific needs or to ask for specific things from others. Western culture frowns upon us having needs and people who express needs are often viewed in a negative way. However, having needs is a part of being human. We, as helpers, can try to offer ourselves in ways that may make this process a little easier for the person who

[2] For more information in communicating with people who are dying or bereaved, see [7].

is grieving. In terms of knowing what to say, when I go to the home of someone who is grieving, I look for photos that may be around the house. I then ask the bereaved individual to tell me a little about the photos, especially if they are of the person who died. I ask about when they were taken, what the bereaved person feels or thinks about as we look at the pictures, and maybe try to open up a discussion about the person who died.

Many bereaved individuals tell me how important it is to be able to say the lost person's name and to talk about the person openly. I try to make it a point to do just that. If I've known the person who died, I try to share some of my own recollections of the person, conversations that we shared, and any details that I can remember in the conversation. If I didn't know the person who died, I'll try to elicit this kind of information from the bereaved individual—What was the person like? What are the things you think about most? What did he or she like to do? In a counseling setting, I call this process "introducing me to your loved one" and I treat it as if the person were having me meet the person who died. I often ask the client to bring in photo albums, pictures, clothing, and linking objects to help in this process. The more they can tell me the better. I ask for more details, allow time for tears if they come, and reflect on the meaning of the lost person in the life of the bereaved individual. This kind of talking also sets the foundation for later conversations, as other things that come up can then be connected to the descriptions of the person and events that were outlined from the beginning.

I also think it is important to drop any preconceived notions about what constitutes support and "grief work" to any individual. If the person comes in and talks conversationally about the weather or about "everyday things," I recognize that it might be very difficult to dive right into the grief process. People are expected to compartmentalize well in our society, and it often can be draining to go from trying to "keep it all together" in the everyday world to "letting it all hang out" in a counseling session. In addition, the time that the person may have set aside to get together may not be when the grief is really "on top," and it may be harder to talk about difficult things when they don't seem as pressing. I often ask people what it's like right before they go to bed, as it seems to universally be a time of connecting with painful images and feelings. I may ask a widow or widower what it's like to come home to an empty house or to eat alone. I may ask a bereaved parent to tell me what it's like for them to go into their child's bedroom. In asking these things, I am not trying to pry. Rather, I am trying to let them know that I will not run away from their pain and am open to *really* knowing how things are going. I then use the responses and cues from the individual to know if she or he is relieved to be able to talk openly or is uncomfortable with the topic, and then try to follow the lead of that person in directing the conversation.

Knowing what community resources are available for grieving individuals can be a big help as well. Where can the person get information on bereavement groups that might be available if he or she is interested in a group? It can be a big relief to a grieving individual to know that he or she is not alone in the grief experience and to hear stories of others who are going through similar challenges after the loss of a loved one. Who can assist with paperwork, address medical or legal issues, or help to learn new skills that used to fall upon the shoulders of the person who died? Are there lectures or educational opportunities about grief or loss that might be helpful? Sometimes, finding books or articles on grief may be helpful, although many bereaved individuals report having a difficult time concentrating on written material and are often too embarrassed to tell you. If you give out information, don't do a "quiz" to see if they've read it. Support may come in offers of a very practical nature—for example, offering to pick up or drive children to an activity, grocery shopping, inviting the person for a meal so that he or she won't have to eat alone, or helping clean the house, or take the car in for service if the person has no energy to do so. I repeatedly hear how much these kinds of gestures mean to my bereaved clients and friends.

As we try to offer ourselves to a grieving individual, we may worry that we aren't doing enough or that we are imposing on the person, or that we are saying all the wrong things. However, what the bereaved individual may notice above everything else we say or do is that we do care and want to be supportive. If we offer ourselves without an expectation of what the response should be and if we are open to hearing from the bereaved person what his or her experience is versus telling him or her what it should be like, then we are giving the best that we can—the gift of unconditional acceptance, empathy, and respect. It is in this environment of support that healing can begin to take place.

REFERENCES

1. S. Caplan and G. Lang, *Grief: The Courageous Journey,* Cor Age Books, London, Ontario, 1993.
2. O. Kroeger and J. Thuesen, *Type Talk,* Bantam Doubleday, New York, 1988.
3. D. Keirsey, *Please Understand Me II,* Prometheus, Del Mar, California, 1998.
4. E. Aron, *The Highly Sensitive Person,* Broadway Books, New York, pp. 3-22, 1996.
5. T. Golden, Men and Grief, in *Readings in Thanatology,* J. D. Morgan (ed.), Baywood, Amityville, New York, pp. 339-345, 1997.
6. J. Oaks, Growing Beyond Survival: Grief Experiences of Children from Dysfunctional Families, in *Personal Care in an Impersonal World,* J. D. Morgan (ed.), Baywood, Amityville, New York, 1993.
7. R. Buckman, *I Dont' Know What to Say,* Key Porter, Toronto, Canada, 1988.

CHAPTER 5

Social Support for Bereaved Children and Teens

Mindy L. K. Gough

It is for them that we often grieve most at the time of a death. The children, whatever the age, are often seen as the most poignant and unfortunate victims of bereavement. And most unfortunately, the bereaved child or teenager often seems beyond the reach of our usual offers of comfort. He does not necessarily appreciate our casserole, brought to lighten the load of the remaining spouse. She may not value our thoughtfully chosen sympathy card with its adult-oriented wording and imagery. He may not understand or feel comforted by our carefully selected words murmured in the visitation line. So what to do? This chapter will offer suggestions for family, friends, neighbors, teachers and school personnel, clergy, youth workers, and anyone else who wishes to reach out to help a child or teenager following a devastating loss.

In these pages, we will assume for the purposes of clarity that the bereaved child is female and that her parent is male. We will also assume that readers are not providing professional grief counseling to the bereaved child, but are people involved in some way in the child's life and wanting to support her.

The first point that must be made clearly is this: children do grieve. If we believe the old notions that children don't understand loss, that children are resilient and bounce back, or that children should be spared the reality of death and shielded from grief, then we ignore the needs of the grieving child. If we choose to think that a child doesn't understand nor grieve following the death of a loved one, we lose an opportunity to provide the comfort we offer his or her parents. If you are going to help a grieving child, you must understand some basic things about grieving children. It is beyond the scope of this chapter to provide these lessons, and readers are therefore directed to the resources listed in the resource list at the end of the chapter. Misunderstanding children's grief-related behavior can lead to hurtful and long-term consequences. Be sure that your efforts at helping are aided by some knowledge about how children typically respond to a loss.

The helper's level of involvement depends to a great extent on his or her pre-existing relationship with the bereaved child. Don't, however, assume that if you aren't close to the child or his family that you can't help. A grieving child often comes from a family consisting of grieving parents, siblings, and grandparents, and your ability to be "outside the situation" may be immensely helpful. Children often fear hurting their grieving relatives further by talking about the loss, and an objective non-grieving helper may be preferred. However, if you are fortunate enough to have developed a friendship or mentoring relationship with a bereaved child prior to his or her loss, you will be in a special position to provide effective support.

Social workers have an oft-quoted maxim; "start where the client is." The helper wishing to assist a bereaved child would do well to heed this advice. Ask the child what she needs. Is she interested in having someone to talk to about her loss? Does she need practical help in memorializing her loved one? Can you drive her to the gravesite for a private visit there? Does she need to forget about her loss for a while? Can you take her to the mall for an afternoon out? Does she need help with her homework? Is she worried about mom or dad? Can you intercede with a grieving parent who is finding it difficult to make objective decisions? Each child will have a different list of needs and desires. The child's response to you will, of course, depend upon her age, her cognitive abilities, and countless other factors.

HELPING THE CHILD BY HELPING HER FAMILY

It is most important for a would-be helper to approach the bereaved child's parent. You must have his permission, first of all, to spend time with his child. Ask him what his child needs, in his view. What has the child been told about the loss? Is there anything that he doesn't want the child to know? In which activities does the parent *not* want his child to participate? For example, does the parent want the child to wait to visit the cemetery until the family can go there together? What are the family's religious views? The parent's wishes, even if he is deeply immersed in his own grief, must be respected. However, if you believe a parent is making decisions that will have harmful effects for his children, talk to other people who are involved with the family. Perhaps an aunt, grandparent, close friend, boss, family doctor, clergy person, or other respected individual can help you to approach the parent with your concerns.

One of the most effective ways to support a grieving child is to support her grieving parent or parents. In situations where a parent's spouse or child has died, the parent may find it very difficult to support his child as he usually does. His own grief may feel too intense, or he may simply not know how to approach his child's pain. Below are a number of ways to help the bereaved child's family. Remember that not all suggestions will fit every situation. You must choose what to do based on your relationship with the child and family, the family's preferences, and the particular circumstances of the loss.

At the time of the death, the family may be in a state of crisis and disorganization, and may question whether to involve the children in what is going on. The helper can gently suggest that child attend the wake and funeral. It is vital that children of all ages be prepared appropriately for the sights, sounds, and emotions they will encounter during the rituals surrounding a death. Johnson et al. give a concise guide to this preparation process (see resource list). You can offer to accompany the child to the funeral and be prepared to go with her if she needs to leave during the service. You might also propose that the children remain involved at an age appropriate level with all of the memorializing and decision-making.

Although it may seem helpful, do not offer to take the children away from the family home during the time after a death. Children need to maintain their physical connection with their remaining family members, even if those people are consumed with grief. It is not beneficial to attempt to hide grief from children—rest assured that most children would be all too aware of the tension and emotion in the home. It is more helpful to talk gently but frankly with the child about why the adults are behaving as they are.

If a parent needs some respite or if there is a particular event that he does not want the child to observe, such as a police interview, you can go to the child's home to spend time with her so the parent can attend to his own needs. You might take the bereaved child for a walk, or a brief, low-key outing. If you are particularly close to the family, you might offer to move in for a few weeks in the role of housekeeper and general supporter *if* this is what the family wants. You might cook, clean, do laundry, run errands, and provide other practical and emotional assistance where it is required. This should not be an ongoing arrangement; after several days or weeks, you can taper off your in-house involvement. Be sure that you don't just leave suddenly.

Do not automatically perform tasks or activities that the parent can and perhaps should do with the children. You may contribute to a sense of powerlessness or helplessness in the parent by doing so, and it is important to remember that such tasks can function as healing activities for the bereaved family. Allow the parent, for example, to help the bereaved child write a letter to the person who has died, or to work with the child to create a memory book. If the parent does not initiate these activities, or feels he cannot participate, you can suggest them and offer to assist the children.

If the parent does not seem aware of the benefits of setting aside some of the belongings of the person who has died, you can suggest this in a respectful way. If the parent does not feel able to go through the deceased person's belongings, you can offer to assist older children to select clothing, tools, knick-knacks and other items that will help them to remember their loved one. It is important, of course, to ascertain ahead of time whether any items are off-limits; perhaps some belongings have been specifically bequeathed or spoken for already. If a child is too young to select for herself, you can offer to choose a variety of special items for her. These can be placed in a well-marked box and put aside to be given to the child later. Remember that keepsake items need not be expensive; one grieving boy I know gained immense comfort from his dad's old t-shirt while another was proud to own his mother's hiking boots.

While it may seem logical or helpful to offer to assist in cleaning the family's home following a death, be sure that you do not remove any of the deceased person's belongings, tidy up his or her room, or even do his or her remaining laundry without asking first. These seemingly mundane household items often symbolize a connection to "normal"—the time before the death tore the child's world apart. A bereaved child may feel violated and angry if she is not ready for these familiar sights to be removed. There is no rush. The helper can kindly remind the parent of this if necessary.

Parents may be bewildered or hurt by the responses of their children, especially if the children appear not to grieve following a death. Your knowledge of children's responses to grief will help you to reassure the parent that the child is grieving in an age-appropriate way. You can remind the grieving parent that it may be most difficult for his child to talk to him about her grief, as many bereaved children fear reopening parental grief wounds by discussing the loss. Grieving parents who bring their children to me for grief counseling commonly state that they just want to determine whether their child's grief is "normal." They tell me that they feel sometimes as though they are not able to neither look objectively at their children's grief nor offer adequate help due to their own grieving. If a bereaved child's parent expresses such sentiments, you can support him in finding a counselor or consultant who is knowledgeable and experienced in working with bereaved children. Often, a single session is all that is required to provide reassurance and suggestions for parents. To find a qualified counselor, ask a trusted funeral home director, palliative care or hospice team member, clergy person, or family physician. Remember that the final decision belongs to the parent; you simply provide a list of names and phone numbers with which he can make his choice.

Sometimes grieving parents slip into a pattern of hypervigilance or become overly protective of their bereaved children, as they fear that these children too may die. Other bereaved parents may unintentionally ignore or neglect their children as the parent flounders in his own grief. Especially for those parents who resist seeking professional advice regarding problems, you as a supportive helper can reflect back to the parent what you see. Using tact and gentleness, you can assist the grieving parent to identify his behavior and to find new ways to interact with his bereaved child.

Finally, help the parent to make his wishes known and respected in the face of well-meaning but potentially hurtful advice from grandparents or other friends and relatives. Frequently the bereaved parent will face a barrage of unsolicited "should's" from a variety of people, some of whom may appear very wise. Commonly offered advice includes, "the children are too young to grieve," "the children shouldn't attend the funeral," and "the children should be sent away." A grieving parent may feel confused and pulled in many directions. You can assist by firmly and kindly re-stating the parent's position to those who offer such counsel, and by providing literature or pamphlets that will educate advice-givers about helping grieving children. See the resource list for examples.

The bereaved child can be helped effectively by the helper willing to look out for her parents. Providing practical help, emotional support, and checking in frequently will not only give some respite to the beleaguered grieving parent but will give the bereaved child reassurance that she and her family are not alone as they mourn.

COMMUNICATING WITH THE GRIEVING CHILD

A grieving child is not necessarily a fragile child; many a youngster has expressed resentment of people who treat them as though they were. However, it is awkward to pretend that nothing has happened. Both you and the bereaved child will be fully aware that a momentous change has occurred. Therefore, it is advisable to be frank but gentle in your approach. Use proper terms to describe what has happened; state that the loved one has died, not "passed away" or "passed on." Do not try to avoid the topic, but do not focus solely on the death either. If "THE DEATH" is the only or usual topic of conversation between you and the child, she will soon find you tiresome.

Children have told me that they take exception to adults who are dramatic, weepy, melodramatic, or always solemn. Children appreciate adults who model an open, honest approach to discussing death, those who don't make death a "touchy" subject. It is a mistake, though, to give a bereaved child more information than she can cope with. Wait until a child asks specific questions before volunteering information, and then keep your explanations simple and age appropriate. If you do not know the answer to a child's question, say so. Avoid using clichés such as, "I know how you feel," "God only takes the best," or "Only the good die young." Aside from the obvious lack of truth contained in these statements, children, especially teens, can be very sensitive to your use of clichés and assumptions.

Be sensitive to the feedback the bereaved child sends your way. If she seems uncomfortable or unaccepting of your overtures, back off but try again in a few days, perhaps with a different approach. For example, if she does not seem interested in talking to you about how she's feeling, you might wait a day or two and then invite her to a sporting event or show. Never hug or touch a child unless you are certain she is comfortable with you doing so.

While you may have a special sensitivity to a child's grief if you have suffered a similar loss, do not assume that your grief and this bereaved child's grief are anything alike. If your parent or sibling died when you were the child's age, you can say so, but be sure not to encumber the child with unresolved grief related to your own loss. If you are feeling very sad about the loss the child has suffered—for example, if her deceased mother was your friend—don't be reticent to display your feelings. Beware, though, of burdening the child with your grief. Remember that you are there to help her, and it is not appropriate to expect her to provide you with comfort.

Bereaved children may act out in a variety of ways as they struggle to cope with the death of a loved one. Give the grieving child some latitude in terms of behavior and school performance, but do maintain the usual routine and boundaries. The structure you provide may help the bereaved child to feel secure in the midst of great instability. Encourage and normalize her grief responses. Help her to understand that grief is a natural outcome after the loss of a loved one. Give her permission to grieve, and discourage her from setting a time limit for her mourning.

PRACTICAL HELP FOR GRIEVING CHILDREN

Your committed presence in the life of a mourning family may be the best gift you can provide. Announce to the bereaved child your willingness to assist in a very specific way—"If you need a ride to hockey practice on Thursday evening, please let me know by lunch time that day," or "I am not good at helping with French homework, but I am a science whiz. If you need a hand with math or science assignments, please call me at home." Provide the child with your phone number on a card and be clear with her about your availability. In the early months following a death, you might offer to arrange rides, babysitting, house cleaning, laundry services, and pool and outdoor maintenance, if you are not able to provide these kinds of assistance.

Let the bereaved child know that she is not responsible for her grieving parents. You might say something like "Your dad will be sad for a long time, and it is O.K. to be sad with him, but it isn't your job to make dad feel better. If you are really worried about dad, call me at this number." Grieving children, especially those who feel the need to fill the role of a missing parent, are often relieved to know that another adult will be watching out for mom or dad. Encourage the child to see her parent's grief as a normal response to the loss that has occurred.

Bereaved children of all ages gain comfort and retain a sense of relationship by keeping tangible mementoes of their loved one. Either on your own or with the child's involvement, gather things that belonged to the deceased person—photographs, poems, awards, recipes, and so on. Seek out the coworkers, neighbors, and friends of the person who died and ask them each to write down one or two special memories or funny stories. With all of these items (or photocopies of them to enable you to create several copies for siblings), make a scrapbook to be bound and presented to the child now or later in her life. You can add your own recollections, if you knew the child's loved one. Again, be sure not to usurp the parent's role in this process as he may wish to work on this project himself.

When you are helping very young grieving children, get down on the floor and play. Offer to take them for daily walks if possible. Accompany them to their usual programs such as day care or swimming class. Be prepared for some heart-wrenching questions and comments from children of this age group. One two and a half year old girl asked her mother, "Did daddy go to work forever?" several weeks after her father's death. Other children in this age group have asked questions that have shocked or horrified the adults in their lives. A naturally curious three year old asked her mother if her brother's head had fallen off yet when they visited the cemetery months after his death. Rehearse ahead of time how you will respond to such questions. It is helpful to use visual and tactile object lessons to discuss death with little children—the crumbling and returning to the earth of the fall leaves, for example, can be used as an analogy for the process of bodily disintegration.

With very young bereaved children, it is of particular importance to discuss with the parent beforehand what the child has been told about the death. Do not confuse or frighten the child by adding new information or contradictory explanations, no matter how strongly you may disagree with what the parent has told the child. If the child asks you a question that you simply cannot answer in the parent's preferred way—for example, when you believe strongly that one's soul lives on after death while the parent has told the child that one ceases to exist at death—you can direct the child back to her parent. You might say something like, "That is something I think you need to talk about with your dad." Regardless of your views, don't critique the bereaved parent's parenting. Undoubtedly he is doing the best he can.

For school aged children, it is helpful to set weekly "dates" to get together. Offer to talk about the death or not talk about it—but give the child your undivided attention for at least an hour or two. Your time together does not have to be terribly exciting. A trip to the library or a walk at the park are both opportunities for the child to be away from her home, to talk if desired, and to be the focus of a caring adult. Additionally, you can have the child help you perform tasks around her home, such as raking leaves, changing a light bulb, and so on. If you have time and the child seems interested, you could work on a project or hobby together—stamp collecting, knitting, photography, or whatever other activity is desired. If the child worked on the project or hobby with the deceased loved one, be careful not to appear to want to take the place of the person who has died or to complete the project, "because mom would have wanted us to." The important factor, of course, is the time you spend with the child, not the activity itself.

School aged children usually enjoy receiving mail or e-mail addressed just to them. Send notes or cards regularly—not sympathy cards, nor long letters, but simple, brief messages to remind the child that you are thinking of her. You can include cartoons, poems, jokes, confetti, photos, stickers, words of encouragement, and whatever else you think will appeal to the bereaved child. Occasionally a thoughtful gift of a special book, craft kit, or keepsake item will be appropriate, but generally letters and cards sent frequently are of more value. You might also telephone every other day for a month or two, then gradually taper off to weekly or monthly check-in calls.

Children in the elementary school grades are often particularly keen to create memorials to their loved ones. With the parent's permission, you can offer to help the bereaved child to create a memorial poem, artwork, or charitable project. A nine-year-old boy was very eager to build a mailbox to hang on his teenaged sister's grave marker for all the letters that her teenaged friends were leaving there. A group of twelve and thirteen year old children put together a small service consisting of poems they had written, popular music, and candle lighting, to honor the younger brother of one of the children. A seven-year-old boy collected pledges for the Terry Fox Run in memory of his father. Use your skills to facilitate a memorial project, but be sure that the bereaved child controls the process.

Although one should not generalize too much, it is fair to say that teenaged mourners usually prefer to talk to their peers about their feelings rather than talking to any adult. However, it cannot hurt to make the bereaved teenager aware of your willingness to listen. With teenagers particularly, you must not push yourself upon them. Ask the grieving teenager what she needs. If your offer of help is given a lukewarm reception or is rejected outright, back away. Continue, though, to offer your presence and assistance in a sensitive, kindly way. Be aware that teenagers can be extremely sensitive and take offense to things you unwittingly do. A teenager might not tell you what you've done to cause affront, but she may later say to friends, "That woman called at the exact time of day that mom died!" or "All she cares about is how my dad is doing," or "She had the audacity to ask me how school was going!" A flexible, friendly, easy going, and tolerant approach is best for teens.

Bereaved teenagers may appreciate a gift of grief-related literature or a grief journal, depending upon the quality and relevance of the book. Avoid books that are written for adults; there are growing numbers of appropriate books written for bereaved teenagers. It is valuable to lessen the pressure on teenagers to be the replacement adult for a deceased parent. Encourage the grieving teen to continue with pursuits typical of teenagers—sports, friends, school, volunteering, and the like—and help her with the practical aspects of these activities. Giving rides, chaperoning, cheering for her team, and helping her prepare a resume are all useful ways to assist. A bereaved teenager may also appreciate your assistance with household responsibilities that she has inherited following the death of a parent.

The value of physical activity for bereaved teenagers (and for younger children) cannot be underestimated. If you are able, take your bereaved teenaged friend out to shoot baskets, play racquetball, go for a bike ride, or whatever activity interests you both. The exercise will benefit the teenager physically and perhaps emotionally, as pent-up feelings of anger and sadness find release. Additionally, a physical activity provides an opportunity for you to be present with the grieving teenager while lessening the potential for awkwardness associated with "just talking."

SCHOOL AND OTHER ACTIVITIES

When a bereaved child returns to school, Girl Guides, or any other group activity for the first time after a death, she may feel very much set apart from her peers. She may wonder how much they know, she may dread having to tell them what has happened, she may fear crying in front of them, or she may have a variety of other emotional responses. You can assist by offering to speak briefly to the group prior to the child's return in order to tell them about the death and give them suggestions for helping the bereaved child feel comfortable upon her return. Encourage the children not to single her out, tease her or treat her differently and alert the teacher to watch for this common behavior. You might also mobilize the child's peers to create cards and letters to express sympathy or welcome her back. Regardless of whether the child wishes you to speak to her peers, it is a good idea for someone to alert the teacher, principal, or group leader to the situation. You might take on this responsibility if the child's parent is in agreement.

You can assist the parent to help the bereaved child to prepare emotionally for her return to her activities. Talk with her about what it will be like. Tell her what her peers have been told. If she feels it will be helpful, you might arrange for her to visit the school building on the weekend prior to her return so that she can experience the environment without the worry of seeing the other children. Discuss the details that will be important to the child—how will she catch up? What has she missed? What will she wear? How will she respond to expressions of condolence? How will she answer questions? Where will she go if she needs to be alone for a moment?

On the grieving child's first day back to school or a group activity, offer to drive or walk with her. It is prudent to tell the child you will wait for a pre-determined time outside the building in case she feels unable to continue, but offer reassurance and confidence in her ability to meet this challenge. Arrange to be waiting outside the building after the school day or activity is finished. For younger children especially, you may wish to offer to accompany them to the classroom or activity until they feel comfortably settled. Older children will likely reject this offer, as your presence will cause them to seem even more set apart from their peers. A daily check-in following the child's return to school can help to ensure that the child is not overwhelmed. Expect a child's academic success to be lessened for the remainder of the school year after the death of a loved one, and intercede with school personnel on the child's behalf if it appears that she will fail a course or grade. Maintaining open communication with the child's teacher can alleviate most academic concerns.

IN THE RELIGIOUS SETTING

A child's return to the church, synagogue, mosque, or other religious setting can be more difficult even than the return to school. If the funeral for the child's loved one was held in the religious setting, she may have a strong aversion to returning there. She may be struggling with her faith because of the loss she has suffered. As with her return to school, you can help the child to prepare emotionally for her return to the religious setting. Offering to provide transportation to and from services is helpful, as is suggesting that she sit with you during the service. For the bereaved child who is feeling very reluctant or distraught about her return, but desires it nonetheless, you might arrange private seating for her in a balcony or office. If it is your religious custom, you may wish to mention the child and her family in the prayers said during the service.

For helpers wishing to provide spiritual support, letting the child know that she is in your prayers is appropriate. Visit her on behalf of the religious community. However, do not offer religious platitudes or pat religious answers such as, "God only gives us what we can handle," as children may resent such statements. Offer literature or point out scriptural references that you think may provide spiritual comfort, but be very careful not to push your religious views and interpretations onto the grieving child. You are better to approach the child in a spirit of love, friendship, and caring and leave religious instruction for a later time.

IN THE MEDICAL SETTING

It is worth mentioning the role of the family physician and his or her staff in the life of the grieving child. Families often turn first to the medical doctor for help, and his or her response may determine whether the bereaved child is supported or left to find her own way through the pain of grief. In the medical setting, support a grieving child by allotting sufficient time to connect with her. Ask how she is doing and watch for non-verbal indications of her inner state. Do not appear rushed; a child is more likely to keep her feelings to herself if she perceives herself as a bother. Educate the child about the grief process and normalize what she is experiencing. Connect her with a skilled counselor if you think she would benefit from professional consultation. In years gone by, medication was often prescribed to alleviate the sadness of grieving people. Remember, though, that sadness following the death of a loved one is absolutely normal and necessary, and do not quickly seek to eliminate it. Instead, offer frequent appointments, reassurance, and encouragement.

YOU, THE SUPPORTER

It can be hard work to support a grieving child or teenager. We feel deep empathy for these young people and wish that they did not have to experience such pain at a tender age. Be kinder than usual to yourself while you are helping a bereaved child. Get lots of rest and decide ahead of time what you can and cannot do. Remember that you are not the only person involved in the grieving child's life. Be sure to enlist the help of all those who care about this child. Maintain your boundaries. You don't have to give all of yourself in order to have a significant impact on a bereaved youngster's life. Finally, allow me to thank you on behalf of the grieving child. She may not have the mental or emotional resources to thank you now, but be assured that your love and involvement will be remembered gratefully for the rest of her life.

RESOURCE LIST

Dougy Center for Grieving Children, The. (1999). *What About the Kids? Understanding Their Needs in Funeral Planning and Services.* Portland, Oregon: The Dougy Center.

Fitzgerald, Helen. (1992). *The Grieving Child: A Parent's Guide.* New York: Fireside.

Goldman, Linda. (1994). *Life and Loss: A Guide to Help Grieving Children.* Muncie, Indiana: Accelerated Development Inc.

Johnson, J. and Roberts, J. (1995). *Thank You For Coming To Say Goodbye.* Omaha: Centering Corporation.

Linn, Erin. (1990). *150 Facts About Grieving Children.* Incline Village, Nevada: The Publisher's Mark.

Matlins, Stuart M. (2000). *The Perfect Stranger's Guide to Funerals and Grieving Practices.* Woodstock, Vermont: Skylight Paths Publishing.

Schaefer, D. and Lyons, C. (1993). *How Do We Tell the Children?: A Step-by-Step Guide for Helping Children Two to Teen Cope When Someone Dies.* New York: Newmarket Press.

Wolfelt, Alan D. (1996). *Healing the Bereaved Child: Grief Gardening, Growth Through Grief and Other Touchstones for Caregivers.* Fort Collins, Colorado: Companion Press.

CHAPTER 6

School Support for Bereavement and Grief

Robert G. Stevenson

The school is a natural support system. The members of a school community typically spend many hours there each week, anywhere from 35 to 70 or more, spread over five to seven days. They maintain contact with members of this "community" at other times as well. They work together, play together, and share the knowledge they gain about life. With such close proximity it is easy to come to know others very well, their strength and weakness, success and failure, happiness and sorrow. Students may say they are there because it is required, that they have no choice. However, this does not explain the many hours spent there with classmates and teachers outside of the regular class hours. It cannot explain why students in some schools who have lost a loved one want to return to the school to be there with their friends and teachers. They return there because they see the school as a place where they will receive support in dealing with the issues in their lives.

Teachers receive a similar support. Educators sometimes find that, having given so many years to their students, it is almost as if the school has become an extension of their own family. They refer to their students as "their kids." Why did these people become teachers? Why did they choose to enter the field of education? It was not for financial profit. Teacher salaries are better than they once were, but there are many ways to earn more in other fields. If an educator tries to answer all of the demands made on him or her, teaching is one of the most demanding. Is it the love of a subject and the chance to keep studying? For people who make this choice, students become only a "distraction." Such "educators" may make a contribution at the University level, or may even write articles to assist other teachers in their work—but they should not be in a classroom unless the needs of their students are their first concern. That is then the answer. Teachers choose this profession to provide their students with information and experiences that will help them deal with the situations they face as they move through life.

Today, dying, death, and grief are life events that many of our students face on a regular basis. Perhaps they always have faced these issues and we have only recently become aware of their effect on students. Some children deal with loss on a DAILY basis. In the United States we have found that as many as:

- 1 in 20 children has a parent die by age 18;
- 1 in 900 high school students dies each year (accident/suicide/homicide/illness);
- some schools experience the death of a teacher or staff member; and
- some students must learn to cope with sibling death (stillbirth, miscarriage), family change (separation/divorce/remarriage), life threatening illness (self or family member), serious physical injury, violence, the fear of violence, and the loss of "security."

Students also undergo:

Emotional numbing—This can vary from a brief period of shock to a reaction where children believe, in effect, that if feelings hurt this much, they will withdraw into themselves and refuse to feel anything at all.

Guilt/anger—These two feelings are often linked in grieving people and may result in apathy (a withdrawing from life) or in acting out. This acting out from guilt and/or anger may be directed at others through verbal or even physical attacks. It can also be directed back at the student him/herself in a pattern of "accidents" or as punishment seeking behavior.

Inability to concentrate—Grieving students may work on assignments, at home or in school, in the same way as they previously did but with results that are far less satisfying. Their minds are, to put it simply, "on other things." Their loss is paramount and academic work takes a back seat or may be dismissed entirely because it has become meaningless in the face of death.

Fear of the future—The future is unknown and children may fear they will be unable to cope with additional losses that could arise in this unknown future. Examples of this fear may be seen in students who resist any further changes in their lives or their environment. The future requires every person to be able to make decisions. No decision can be better than the information upon which it is based. If we want our students to be able to make effective decisions for their own lives, we need to include information about loss and grief in their knowledge base.

In examining the school as a support in times of loss and grief, there are two concepts whose meaning must be clearly understood—bereavement and grief.

Bereavement is the forcible loss of someone or something precious. It is an event, a moment in time. It occurs and is then in the past. *Grief* is a *process* by which we learn to include that loss, and others connected with it, in our lives. Learning to grieve effectively—even ONCE—gives a person a vital life skill. In my experience as a teacher, this skill is every bit as important as mathematics or language.

A curriculum is a "statement of priorities." The curricula in our schools reflect what we hold most important. In many countries, classes, units, and curricula that deal with loss and grief have come to be known as "death education." This title is really too narrow. In "death education" courses we help students to learn to deal with losses of all types. However, "death education" is used so widely that it is better to understand its full meaning than to change it to "loss education," even though that is what it has now become.

It can be stated with certainty that a single loss, such as the death of a student, teacher, parent, sibling, or community member, can effect the function of a school. The losses mentioned above will certainly affect the function of any school in which they occur. The impact of loss and death in a school may:

- impair the academic performance of students;
- shorten the attention span of students; and
- cause behavior "problems," such as attention-seeking (or punishment seeking) behavior, acting-out, apathy (withdrawal from life), behavior that copies an absent loved one, a drop in grades, and/or poor health (with frequent absence or visits to the school nurse or to a doctor).

These student reactions are further complicated when their expression is delayed.

In young people, it is not unusual in some cases for such a delay to last as long as five years. It then may be quite difficult to understand the change in a child's behavior, especially when a teacher does not know of the effects caused by the death so many years ago. Furthermore, one affected child can produce a disruptive pattern that can impact on an entire class and one such class can have an impact on an entire school.

We cannot shield our children from loss or from grief. However, there are things we can do that may help to keep those effects from being worse than they otherwise have to be. There are some teachers who hold back because they fear doing or saying something that might make a situation worse. In some places it is said, "It is better to say nothing than to say the wrong thing." A more cruel form of the same idea says, "It is better to remain silent and be thought a fool than to speak up and remove all doubt." Teachers do not remain silent because they do not care about their students. We may remain silent because we DO care, and because we care we do not want to make a difficult situation worse. On this point I wish to be most emphatic. **It is better to *try* to say the right thing, than to say nothing because of worry about saying the wrong thing.** When a caring adult says or does *something* it is always better than saying or doing nothing.

The emotions of "normal" grief include helplessness, hopelessness, and loneliness. These are three of the four emotions present in suicide attempts—the other is a feeling of worthlessness. A teacher's silence can reinforce these very feelings of worthlessness (the child does not deserve help) and helplessness or hopelessness (there is nothing that even an adult can do). There is no guarantee that our words or actions will help a particular child, however silence can create even greater risks for that child. In support of this position I would quote a fellow "educator," Mohandus K. Gandhi. Gandhi once said, "What we can do, we must try to do." It is TRYING that is required. Success, when it occurs, is a bonus.

Sandra Elder, who helped found school support groups in a number of Canadian secondary schools, expressed this quite clearly when she said, "Grief is a human process to be experienced. It is *not* an illness to be treated. It is important to learn to grieve, as it is to learn arithmetic, language, or science. Children witness and feel changes in their lives, often without the skills to express their fears and pain. Grief is a life skill to be learned and lived."

Everything that lives will one day die. Death is, after all, a part of life. Until recently, however, a look at our schools could make one question this basic fact. The topic of death is one that was seldom discussed in schools and some educators labored under the mistaken belief that it is not a subject that they needed to address. Schools often do not have a procedure for coping with student grief. Some teachers are still unaware of the role they can play in helping grieving students. However, the number of educators who have come to see the school as a support system for its members, with *all* of the issues they face, is increasing. The reality is that students do experience the death of loved ones and their grief can have an impact on their learning and on the learning atmosphere that can be real, immediate, and profound.

We know that, when dealing with grief, students may react in any of a variety of ways. Grief, although a healing process, does produce anxiety in the grieving individual and may impact friends and classmates as well. The effects of anxiety on schoolwork have been demonstrated by a number of researchers [see 1, 2]. Students experience a shorter attention span and difficulty in concentrating which may be accompanied by a drop in grades. In varying degrees, many of these students perceive themselves to be "helpless" in coping with crises. They may show signs of depression, increased episodes of daydreaming, or they may withdraw from socialization with peers. These students also report somatic complaints more often than their peers. All of these possible disruptions in the learning process and classroom routine make a teacher's role more difficult. Ignoring these very real difficulties being encountered by students will only magnify their effect. Although many of the tasks connected to coping with grief take place following a death, the time to prepare to carry out these tasks is before the death occurs.

GUIDELINES FOR SCHOOL SUPPORT

The following practical responses have all been used by schools and may serve as a guide to help create a truly supportive atmosphere for those members of the school community dealing with loss. These are not just things to do after a loss. If implemented in advance, their presence helps the school community to fulfill its role as a support system for each of its members. These recommendations can be implemented now in schools to prepare for the time when they will be needed.

Know What Support Exists

In many areas there are now organizations with programs that provide assistance for just this type of situation. The Association for Death Education and Counseling (ADEC), based in the United States, has provided help in creating an atmosphere of support in schools following a loss. They are an important resource for educators. The Rainbows program, founded by Suzy Yehl Marta, is used in homes and schools across the United States to join family and educators in support of the young people both seek to support. In Athens, Greece, Merimna is an organization that has begun to train educators from throughout Greece so that these men and women can be a source of support to their colleagues, their students, and their communities. In Canada, John Morgan established the King's College Center for Education About Death and Bereavement in London, Ontario. The Center sponsors annual conferences on aspects of loss and grief. In British Columbia, Sandra Elder helped found Living Thru Loss, an organization that helps run support groups for bereaved students in schools. Concerned adults should learn about such programs, where they are and how they can be contacted should the need arise.

Have a Procedure in Place to Inform the Class as Soon as Possible When a Death or Other Loss Occurs

In the United States, this was thought to be so important that the National Association of Secondary School Principals established a system for informing the school community of a death [3]. The news will be painful no matter what is done; however, prior planning for such an event can help keep that pain to a minimum by avoiding mistakes—usually well-intentioned—that could make the reaction worse. This is important for children of all ages.

Find a Place in Your Curriculum for Issues Connected to Loss and Grief

Loss education occurs regularly for our students. They see it in their lives and those of their friends. What is needed is not such informal "education" but information delivered in a systematic, measurable way. As was said earlier, a curriculum is a statement of priorities. Find ways to include necessary information about loss, grief, and coping in the formal curriculum. It could be in the form of stories or myths and the values and behavior they teach. It might be in the science classes of older students. It might be through art—studying the art of others or in creating art of the student's own design. Or, it could be through a specific course in death education. I designed and taught such a course, called Contemporary Issues In Life and Death, through the social science department of my school for 25 years. The course was originally called Perspectives on Death, but the title was changed because some school board members were made uncomfortable by the word "death." Using the word "loss" in place of death would not change the content of such a course and could help its acceptance by administrators and members of the board of education. The course was created initially in response to the students' need to have their questions about life and death addressed. The response to their questions included teachers, parents, religious leaders, and academicians from the fields of sociology, psychology, history, and the health sciences.

Over one hundred students took the course, ages 15 to 19, each year—over 3,000 students in all. In all that time there was not a single negative reaction to the course from any student or parent. The course met for four hours of classroom instruction each week and lasted for 18 weeks. It was an elective course that could be chosen by any of the 500 sophomores, juniors, and seniors in our school. About 75 percent of the students chose to take the course. Scheduling conflicts kept some from actually being enrolled, but over 60 percent of the total student body had taken the course by the time they graduated. Please note that the course was not required. My personal belief is that, even though this information may be important at some time to everyone, individual life situations can make it difficult for some to face such an emotional topic at a time not of the student's choosing. Several of the students who did not take the class in high school did take a similar course with me in an evening class at a nearby college. The course had several overall objectives, including:

- assisting students to develop realistic and objective attitudes that view death as an experience common to all living things;
- increasing student awareness of some of the contributions of science and art to our understanding of life and death;
- providing students with information and experiences related to the social, psychological, biological, and economic impact of a death;
- assisting students in differentiating between "normal" and destructive grief;
- presenting current research related to suicide and suicide prevention, including the role of the "gatekeeper" in suicide prevention;
- aiding students to increase internal feelings of control over their lives and helping them to develop effective coping strategies for dealing with losses of all types;

- aiding students in developing their academic skills (such as written expression and vocabulary enrichment), cognitive skills (such as cognitive development, interpretation of data, and application of generalizations),[1] and the important skill of effective communication (of feelings as well as of thoughts).

Encourage Parents to Deal at Home with Issues Related to Loss

In most cases, children will feel more comfortable discussing a loss with their parents who, after all, know their own children better than any "experts." This is an area where the home and school should cooperate to reinforce each other as all parties try to help the children involved. This is not an "either . . . or" situation. Many children need care in all areas of their lives when trying to cope with a major loss, such as with the death of a loved one. It is always appropriate for a parent to tell a child what s/he believes about an afterlife and to pass on personal and family traditions of faith. Such lessons cannot be taught in a public school setting without the risk of violating the personal beliefs of many families. Students can speak of their beliefs, but that is not the same as a presentation by a caring adult who can answer the "Why?" which often follows such explanations. The decision of what to say about a death and when to say it is one that is best made by a parent. However, if parents avoid facing this issue, children may call upon educators for answers to their questions.

Myra Lipman of the New York Parents League has stated (quoted in [4]) that "schools cannot assume the entire responsibility for a child's death education nor can they ignore the matter entirely. There should be effective home-school communication so that parents know what information is being presented to their children." Successful death education courses exist across the country and can make the school a focal point for helping concerned parents with specific needs to contact appropriate support groups in their community.

Provide Role Models in the School

Parents, teachers, and other concerned adults model ways to deal with loss and sadness. They can show children that grief hurts, tears are "normal," and that emotions need not be "avoided." Such an experience can reduce fears of both children and parents and is really effective teaching.

[1] These skills—cognitive development, interpretation of data, and application of generalizations—are based on the work of Hilda Taba in the 1960s and early 1970s. They are intended to assist students in developing their higher-level thinking skills.

Avoid Silence

Social critic Phyllis Schlafly has been quoted as saying, "Anything they (teachers) do is apt to be far worse than doing nothing at all" (quoted in [5]). It has been shown that silence can magnify the feelings of helplessness, hopelessness, and loneliness that are part of all grief reactions and can add feelings of worthlessness [3]. In this way, "silence" may actually strengthen all four of the emotions present in many suicide attempts. The silence that Ms. Schlafly sees as preferable can cause children to feel they must confront alone the topics of loss, dying, death, and the feelings they generate.

Be Aware of the Importance of Nonverbal Communication

All of us must be aware of the many ways in which we communicate. Our attempts to speak with children can be influenced by location (where we speak), time (when we speak), and space (distance between us as we speak). We should be aware of all of the factors that have an impact on our communications with children. Location should be one in which children feel most comfortable or least threatened. In school, this is typically the child's classroom, not an auditorium, cafeteria, or assembly hall. The best time to speak about a death is as soon as the entire staff has been informed and knows what to tell students about what has happened. It is not good to postpone such communication, but it can also be a mistake to speak out too quickly and spread misunderstanding or rumor.

Create Rituals to Acknowledge the Reality of the Changes That Have Taken Place Because of a Loss

Such rituals or memorials need not be traditional or formal, but it is important to show students that a change such as a death does not simply happen without other changes taking place as well. By taking time to mark that change with some ritual, some rite of passage, we confirm that this change has happened and that the child's reactions to that change are justified. If we try to "deny" that a change has taken place, we should not be surprised when children adopt coping mechanisms that attempt to do the same and continue that "denial." In some cases, students may act out to block "business as usual" until some recognition of the death takes place in the school. There are some who believe that such memorials should not take place when a suicide has occurred. There has still been a change for students. One must be careful not to romanticize the method of death but a rite of passage is still essential both to acknowledge the change that has occurred and to validate to students that *every* life has meaning and their absence would be noticed because their life in that school is so important.

When rituals take place in a school following a major loss, such as a death, parents should be kept informed of all that takes place so that they can remain the primary support for their children. Classroom rituals have involved lighting candles, drawing pictures, sharing memories, or, in the case of a student death, creating a memory book as a gift for the parents and family. Other rituals may involve donation of books or other equipment to the school in the name of the deceased (with an accompanying ceremony), or a gift to charity in the name of the deceased. On a personal note, I would suggest that planting a tree may be a good idea but it can be a two-edged sword. What happens when some time later, even years later, these students return to see the tree damaged or even gone entirely. This can actually stir up many painful feelings.

Give Abstract Concepts Some "Concrete" Form

Often some small item can provide comfort and courage to grieving students. A cross, a polished stone, a doll or some other object can be an amulet (warding off evil) or a talisman (helping the possessor to accomplish some difficult task). I have used a plastic "lens" to explain to students how an event can be a lens that changes the way the world looks. Using this lens (which multiplies and rearranges the image in front of them) is a concrete way to explain what happens when we grieve or when we suffer from a loss or other sudden change in our lives. The power in an object or a ritual comes not from the thing itself, but from the caring person who introduces it and from the way in which it is used. If nothing else, it serves as a reminder to the students that there are still people who care about them and are still there to help them if they are needed.

Encourage Helping Others as a Way to Overcome Feelings of Helplessness or Worthlessness

My students used to raise money with candy sales in school. The money was regularly sent to local charities, such as the "Tomorrow's Children's Fund" or the "Emmanuel Cancer Foundation" in the name of deceased loved ones. A notification was then sent to survivors that a gift had been made in their loved one's name. This ritual had benefits at many levels and continued at the students' request for several years. It was important enough to my high school students that they continued it even after my retirement. They also wrote, and had published, a series of articles for other young people by young people on topics such as children attending funerals, teachers' help for grieving students, euthanasia, and grief that follows a death from AIDS. They learned they did not need to listen only to "others." Their opinions had enough value that they, themselves, could *be* "others" offering help to their peers.

Some schools close when a major loss or death occurs. I strongly suggest that this *not* be done. Schools can be, and should be, a place of support for all members of a school community. Closing a school is almost a form of denial, a way of saying that a school has nothing to offer at a time like this. However, students who have suffered a loss increasingly look to their friends and teachers as an important part of their support system in times of crisis. I have even seen students attend school, at least for a time, on the same day as a wake or funeral because it is there they feel "safe" from what has happened to them in the outside world. Do not cut them off from this support.

Offer Support for All Ages

The students in my death education class published several articles discussing what schools could do for students—from a student perspective. We regularly received calls from parents and organizations throughout the area that wanted help for bereaved children and families and wanted to ask my students (high school juniors and seniors) to suggest or to evaluate a particular response. It is clear that schools do not have all the answers to any problem, but they do have information that many parents find useful. When the school can act as a clearinghouse for such information, there is no need to reinvent the wheel.

Provide Security and Structure

With one part of life "out of control" because of a loss, students need to be able to feel that they still have some control in other areas of life. It is not unusual for students to attend class immediately after a loss and to try to go through the day in as "normal" a manner as possible. This gives them a feeling of "control" over this part of life. However, to force children to behave in a routine manner after a death or other major loss, when they do not wish to do so, removes the very feelings of control we are trying to reinforce. Additionally, policies that seek complete control over students to answer some real or imagined threat may, by themselves, push some students toward violent or destructive behavior. Tactics such as "lockdown" try to prevent violence by finding and eliminating contraband. The lockdown does not stop all violence in prisons; neither does it eliminate weapons and contraband. How can it be effective for a school? An "individual" person must *always* be more important that a "general" policy and each student must be aware that this is true.

Plan to Cover a Full Range of Possible Responses

Planning should be directed not only at school-wide response after a death or other loss but at things a teacher may do with an individual student. Teachers should know that an individual child might have an increased need for attention. If asked questions by students, teachers should be honest and avoid platitudes, avoid speaking of blame for the death, listen (and not feel the need to try to solve all of the grieving student's problems or to make everything "all right"). Help students to understand grief and to set priorities. Lower grades do not necessarily make someone a "bad" person. Problems are easier to face and overcome when the student begins to understand the factors that may be causing them.

Help Each Child at His/Her Own Developmental Level

There are materials available to help students understand and cope with loss. Books about losses, such as death and divorce, exist in abundance. They are geared to many ages, developmental levels, and even to specific cultural/ethnic groups. A book that is very good for a middle school student or class may miss the mark entirely if read to second graders. Teachers and parents should know *in advance* what is contained in any story they share with a child. There are death/loss curricula for high schools, middle schools, and elementary schools. These are not automatically interchangeable. Material aimed at younger students can be used with older students, but the reverse is not equally true. A classic book that pointed out the developmental differences in student grief and highlighted possible ways of dealing with grief in ways appropriate to the level of the student is *Discussing Death* by Gretchen Mills [6]. It does not provide a curriculum, but offers instead the information that can be the basis for creating classes to aid grieving students.

Help to Externalize Thoughts and Feelings

Provide ways for students to "get out" the thoughts and feelings they may otherwise keep bottled inside. Drawing pictures, writing, reading stories related to loss or grief (called "bibliotherapy"—book therapy—by some), or telling a story can all be helpful techniques in giving grieving students an opportunity for needed catharsis—an emotional cleaning out. One exercise my students found most helpful was the burning of "secrets." Each student was given a paper. They were asked to write on that paper something they wished to "leave in the past." Or, they could write down (externalize) some secret they felt they could not share with anyone else. Each student was asked to write "something"—no matter what—so that those with items to get rid of would not feel singled out. They could write something important to them, or just write that they had nothing to say.

The papers were then crumpled into balls and placed in a small can (with holes punched at the bottom). They were taken outside and then burned as a way of getting rid of any bad feelings connected with the thought the student had written down. The first time I tried it I was not sure precisely how the students might react. They insisted on watching until they were sure that there was nothing left but ashes. From that day on, every class asked when they too could have that special class. It seems that more students than we realize have painful thoughts and feelings they are looking for a way to "release." (NOTE: This exercise has been used with children ages 8 and older. With young children, it is important to take all necessary time to include a warning about safety. Explain that they should only do this with adults to help.)

Acknowledge That the Impact of a Loss on Students May Effect Their Teachers as Well

As time passes, most members of the school community will grieve, recover, and move on from a loss and its aftermath. It may seem that, since the death of a student has a clear impact on that child's teacher, to stress this point is only to belabor the obvious. However, teachers in the roles of caregiver and educator may have difficulty taking time to tend to their own needs. When a child dies, teachers often spend long hours helping children and parents and in seeking training to be more effective in that role. Such a death also places an emotional strain on teachers as well as on students and parents. It is important that schools acknowledge this situation and that they take time to acknowledge the change that has occurred for staff as well as for students.

Assume a Partnership Role

The partnership of parents and teachers and other members of the community at large are vital in assuring a caring atmosphere for students in which learning can flourish. In addition, every teacher and school should have another "partner" when called on to assist students following a death. Each school should develop a "partner" school that can be called upon for help when a death or other loss affects a school community. Typically such a partnership involved joint staff development so that the educators in both schools get to know each other before some crisis occurs. They then can work out ways in which the school coping with the aftermath of a death can draw on needed support from the partner school. Teachers too may at times need a partner. A teacher coping with personal losses may not be able to give full attention to the needs of grieving students and may require the assistance of a colleague at such a time. Partners can also discuss and evaluate attempted interventions and constantly improve their ability to assist students.

CONCLUSION

There is no one way to assist students . . . no one way to best deal with loss or the grief that follows. These last two examples were written by my students (ages 15–18) and left as a "gift" for future classes. I now share their gift with you.

* * *

STUDENT WRITING #1

Grief: Surviving and Moving On

Grief hurts. Our experience has shown that the following steps MAY prove helpful for people coping with the grief that follows a loss:

- Accept the loss—be tolerant of perceived shortcomings (in yourself as well as others): short temper, avoidance, lack of emotion (that others show), short attention span, lack of energy.
- Be aware of feelings—fear, anger, and guilt (whether real or imagined). We cannot control our feelings but we also do not need to be controlled by them once we accept that they are there.
- Speak about the loss (if you are able)—be patient with misstatements by you or by others.
- Keep busy—but not too busy. Grief can be tiring and you will need your energy.
- Take care of yourself, get sleep, eat sensibly, and get exercise.
- Externalize your grief (through symbols, journals, or sharing with others in some way).
- Accept your understanding of the death (eventually you will need to stop asking "Why?").
- Draw on your personal spiritual background.
- Understand, but do not ignore, negative coping by yourself or others (anger, humor, self-injury, denial, apathy).
- Time can aid healing, but it is NOT automatic—there are times when "professional" help is best (mental health professionals, counselors, religious advisors).
- Utilize every resource available—books, art, and activities—try them all.
- Listen to all those who want to help and be there for those you love.
- Remember, There is NO ONE ANSWER.

* * *

STUDENT WRITING #2

What Students Want/Need

[The following 10 suggestions were originally written by my teenage students for the teachers of a nearby school district following a series of three (unrelated) deaths of students in that school.]

What do we, your students, want? We can tell you. We want to:

- Talk about the death and allow us to initiate discussion when we feel the "need."
- Understand that we may not all want or need to take part in talks or memorials. Please be sure that there is a different place for us to go at that time.
- Provide us with a "safe place" and allow us to go there when we need to.
- Allow for change/continuity in the environment (with a place for student wishes to be expressed).
- Recognize that violence is an outlet that some students will choose for their anger.
- Emphasize that at some point it is OK to get on with life, but this point may be different for each of us.
- Provide us with a contact place (or phone #) when someone may not be otherwise available.
- Listen to us because we are often the ones who know best what we need, even if we can't always find the words to express it.
- Don't try to limit the pain by "labeling" those students who are "really" grieving. It won't make things better and it may make them worse.
- Don't impose cultural "limits" on our expression of grief.
- Never underestimate the power of LOVE (family, friends, faith).

RECOMMENDATIONS

Children who have suffered a major loss clearly have special needs. A well-known psychologist once said of her own grief, that "knowing why you hurt doesn't make it hurt less." It should be added, however, that such knowledge could keep you from hurting more than you have to. If this is true for adults, it is even more so for bereaved children who have lost someone precious to them. To keep the hurt from being worse than it has to, schools and parents have found it helpful to create procedures to employ when the need arises. In this way, plans are formed when the pressures of time and emotional distress are at a minimum. School policies, staff training programs, and even appropriate readings for use by (or with) students can be put in place in advance of need. This is not "therapy." These steps may have a therapeutic effect on some students, but actual therapy is work best left to heath care professionals. In teaching these things we accomplish something else. When we teach students about loss and grief we do not cure emotional illness. What these lessons can "cure" is ignorance and the pain such ignorance may cause.

There are things that can be done by parents and educators now to help children faced with the need to cope with loss. If, as a parent or educator, you had been faced with one of the situations described in this chapter, what would you have done? If you are able to take the time now to think of an answer to that question, it may be the first step toward helping a student in the future.

REFERENCES

1. E. Gaudry and C. Speilberger, *Anxiety and Educational Achievement,* J. Wiley and Sons, Sydney, Australia, 1971.
2. R. Behrens, M. Craushaar, C. Rohrbough, and E. Rosenberg, A Descriptive Study of Elementary School Children Who Have Suffered a Major Loss, Master's thesis, Simmons College of Social Work, 1964, cited by H. Moller in *Explaining Death to Children,* E. A. Grollman (ed.), Beacon Press, Boston, Massachusetts, 1967.
3. R. G. Stevenson and H. L. Powers, How to Handle Death in the School, in *Education Digest,* May 1987.
4. R. G. Stevenson and E. P. Stevenson (eds.), *Teaching Students about Death: A Comprehensive Resource for Educators and Parents,* Charles Press, Philadelphia, Pennsylvania, 1996.
5. F. M. Bordewich, Mortal Fears, *The Atlantic,* February 1988.
6. G. Mills, R. Reisler, Jr., A. E. Robinson, and G. Vermizye, *Discussing Death,* ETC Publishing, Palm Springs, California, 1976.

CHAPTER 7

Acknowledging the Masculine and Feminine in Offering Support

Thomas Golden

Once upon a time life had a general rule that everyone could live by. The Golden Rule very simply and effectively stated that we should "Do unto others as you would have others do unto you." For generations, this adage guided our actions. If we wanted to be treated in a certain way, it was fair to assume that others would also welcome that treatment. In today's world, however, things are not always that simple. Our next-door neighbors are likely to be from a country halfway around the world; gone are the days of homogeneity and uniformity of culture, and with them our safe assumptions about how to treat others.

Diversity is no longer a buzzword, but the reality of our lives. A quick survey of the many ethnic restaurants flourishing in the cities and even small towns of America—sushi, Thai, Jamaican, Ethiopian, and Indian—confirms that our opportunities for and likelihood of encountering different cultures are steadily increasing. We are beginning to learn of traditions and ways of behavior that are quite different from our own. We can envision circumstances in which following the Golden Rule could be ill-advised or even insulting. For example, I recently met via e-mail a person who explained that our tradition of neighbors and friends bringing food to a bereaved household is the opposite of what is observed in Taiwan. There, it is the responsibility of the grieving family to provide food for their visitors. If we were in Taiwan and wanted to be of support to a mourning family, knowing of this cultural difference would allow us to avoid an inappropriate and ineffectual gesture of sympathy.

The same holds true for individual differences. In order to be of support to anyone, you first need to know what that individual would find helpful. Thus, in order to talk about men and how they can be "supported," we need first to look at how they are unique and how this difference may impact the ways we choose to be of support to them.

In my work with men healing from loss, I learned early on that the differences I saw as compared to women were more related to a difference in masculine/feminine than to a difference in male/female. By this I mean that I learned that men and women both have the masculine and feminine energies, and that it was a matter of how much of each an individual had that made the difference. In general, men tend to have more of the masculine energy and women more of the feminine, but there are plenty of exceptions. There are many men with large doses of feminine energy and also many women with an abundance of the masculine. It isn't a matter of male and female being the dividing line, but rather an individual's unique blend of the masculine/feminine energies that sets us apart.

I once gave a workshop at a conference on diversity and culture. Of the numerous cultures represented, I had been asked to represent "masculine culture," and a woman asked to represent "feminine culture." This conference had it right. They realized that in so many ways we live in different cultures as masculine and feminine. They recognized that the difference wasn't as much about men and women as it was about the masculine and the feminine.

I think the same is true for how we find support helpful. Some women may find the masculine ways of being supported more harmonious with their nature, and many men may experience the opposite. To complicate matters further, certain situations and certain times in our life might call for more of the masculine or more of the feminine. I have found that knowing our own unique balance of masculine/feminine is a sign of maturity and a big help in understanding our own nature and accepting differences in others.

So our first task in beginning to unravel the mysteries of how to support someone with an abundance of masculine energy is to get to know the masculine. Objects that are long and lean are the traditional symbols of the masculine: the sword, the spear, the scepter, the magician's wand, the king's staff, and the phallus. These objects are often pointed, and, like the arrow or the spear, intended to move in only one direction. This can be contrasted with the traditional symbols of the feminine: round, inclusive, and holding, such as the bowl. Very different from the masculine image of one object going toward one target! The masculine tends to be interested in goals, products, efficiency, and outcomes, while the feminine tends to find greater interest in relationships, intimacy, and "containers."

These characteristics of masculine and feminine can play themselves out in many areas of daily life. We could define a room by its blend of masculine and feminine qualities, for instance. A masculine room might be long and narrow with all the seats pointed in one direction toward a podium. A female room might be designed in the round, with seats facing each other to offer plenty of opportunity for interaction.

Another example of the masculine side often appears during family vacations taken by automobile. The person with the greater amount of masculine will usually want to take the most direct route. Like the spear or arrow, he or she wants to go straight to the goal and lacks interest in side trips and collecting souvenirs along the way. These activities are seen as distractions and impediments to the actual goal of arriving at the destination. The person with the greater feminine is likely to be more interested in the side paths along the way and the stories behind them. Like the bowl, he or she will be less focused on the "goal" of getting there and more interested in collecting memories and memorabilia of the journey.

We can take this example a step further by looking at typical masculine and feminine mental activities that people use to entertain themselves on auto trips. When on a trip I pass the time by doing mental calculations about our progress. Having noted our time of departure and the number of miles we have traveled, I do mental math to find our average speed and then calculate our estimated time of arrival. I enjoy this. It's like a game to me, and I often will do the mental math on the hour or the half hour in order to make the computations a bit simpler. This makes the trip seem to go by a bit faster, and keeps me occupied in an enjoyable manner. This is a typical masculine, goal-focused activity. On the other hand, while my daughter knows a good deal more mathematics than I and could just as easily engage in this sort of mental math, she chooses to make the time flow by reading romance novels. She becomes captivated in a story that swirls around relationship and intimacy. This choice is not a matter of intelligence or knowledge, but has to do with our mental framework and the activity that most pleases our nature. For me, it is related to the goal of arriving at our destination. For my daughter, it is being involved in stories. My son, however, couldn't care less about the math or the stories. He gets completely absorbed in video games where he is trying to compete and WIN! His activity has to do with the masculine aspects of goals, production, and output. But it could just as easily have been my daughter who preferred the video games. Again, it is not so much a matter of gender as it is our own unique nature and our inclination toward masculine or feminine.

There are many other differences that stem from our balance of masculine and feminine. The linguist Deborah Tannen has categorized them by keywords. For the masculine she uses the keyword "independence," and for the feminine she uses the keyword "intimacy." Tannen points out that these differences are not exclusive; women have an interest in independence and men have an interest in intimacy. But the man's "primary lens" for viewing the world is usually one of independence, while a woman is more likely to see the world through a lens of intimacy. For men, this mode of independence is part of what is termed the "hierarchical view" of the world as discussed in this excerpt from *Swallowed by a Snake*:

> Men tend towards a hierarchical nature, viewing the world in terms of who is governing whom. Women, on the other hand, tend to view the world through the lens of who is relating to whom. Tannen points out that men live in a hierarchical world that is characterized by having the consciousness of who is "one up" or "one down." Conversations are seen by men as a place to maintain

> their image and to avoid being put into a one down position, with the goal of maintaining their independence. It is easy to see this developing in boys as they learn in grade school to put each other down. A great deal of effort and energy goes into creating and remembering put downs in order to be ready for the word battle that goes on between boys. This is the beginning of hierarchy. It can also be seen in the knowledge that each young boy has about who in his class can kick the farthest, run the fastest, etc. The hoped for goal of the boy and later the man is to appear to be on top of things and, above all, maintain independence [1].

The difference between the masculine primary lens and the feminine primary lens has direct consequences for our efforts to provide appropriate support. The first element of all healing is safety, and people who see the world through a primary lens of independence will find safety in very different places than those who see the world through a primary lens of intimacy. If you value independence and have a hierarchical view of the world, you will be unlikely to want to share your problems. Sharing with those above you on the governing ladder would make you look considerably less independent, yet you also don't want to share with those below you on the hierarchy since you don't feel that your problems are their responsibility. People with a strong masculine are more inclined to handle problems alone, which often results in a more quiet and solitary form of healing. Add to this the shaming that our culture puts onto males who express sadness in public and you have a strong case for men to prefer a more introverted form of healing.

Women, however, tend to live in a network of support. Their concern is not so much to appear independent, but to seek connection with their peers whom they view from a position of being equal rather than from a hierarchical standpoint. Their negotiations are more for closeness, both seeking and giving confirmations of support, rather than maintaining status. It's easy to see that those comfortable with a keyword of intimacy would likely find it safe and productive to share their grief with the people around them.

Masculine and feminine differences also can be discovered by observing where and how men bond with other men and women bond with other women. The men will tend to bond by being shoulder-to-shoulder and working toward a common goal. You can easily think of places where this happens, from the fire department to the battlefield, to fishing together or being on a sports team. It's interesting to note that the more dangerous the goal the deeper the bond seems to be. Being shoulder-to-shoulder means we're on the same team, whereas facing someone often means conflict. The "enemy" is the one you have to "face." This, of course, has impact when we expect eye contact from men. For them, facing someone has millions of years of genetic coding that says, "This means battle!" Conversely, women tend to view facing someone as a means to deepen intimacy. When the bowl is your symbol, facing each other is a standard expectation. In fact, to not face someone can be interpreted as being isolating or ostracizing. Thus, we see that the masculine and feminine viewpoints can convey very different concepts for the same event.

If the natural mode of the masculine is shoulder-to-shoulder, then we may assume that is where those who have a predominance of masculine will feel most comfortable and safe, the place that feels like "home." As we have said, a feeling of safety is an important component of supporting someone. People generally don't heal in a foxhole. When we are in the midst of chaos or confusion we generally don't move toward wanting to heal. It is only when we begin to feel safe and more stable that we find the energy to begin to heal. Traditional psychotherapy, based on face-to-face sharing of intimate details, tends therefore to be a place much more friendly to the feminine rather than the masculine. But this is due not only to the fact that the masculine is more comfortable with shoulder-to-shoulder rather than face-to-face, but also because the masculine prefers to focus on the future rather than the past. Interested in goals, product, independence, efficiency, and output, the masculine is pulled toward the future. The past has nothing to do with goals and outcomes, and many with a strong masculine side will scoff at talking about the past because "there is nothing you can *do* about it." For the masculine, the past serves only to help us understand where we need to point our energies. The past is the antithesis of the masculine pull toward outcome and goals. It's the future that interests the masculine because you can do something about it

Among the reasons why men and women find different paths to heal is that we are physically different. Not better or worse, just different. New research shows that our brains respond differently when given the same mental task. Asked to rhyme certain words, men's and women's CT scans showed very different brain activity. The men's scans showed activity in just one area of the brain, while the women's scans showed simultaneous activity in a variety of places in the brain. As opposed to the single lit area of a man's brain, a number of areas of the brain lit up as a woman performed the rhyming task. Again, we can think of the spear versus the bowl—the man's brain moving to one spot and the woman's brain employing many areas.

Another physical difference is that women tend to have more prolactin, a pituitary hormone that aids in our access to emotional tears. The more prolactin you have, the easier your access to emotional tears, and the less you have, the more difficult it will be to cry. Men tend to have less prolactin than women since male production of the hormone decreases after puberty, leaving men less able to access emotional tears. The importance of this is that a man may very well have strong sadness, but not have as many tears as his female counterpart. The general rule is that you can never gauge a man's pain by the number of tears he sheds.

The corpus callosum, the small band that runs between the two hemispheres of the brain, is yet another area of physical difference between men and women. A woman's corpus callosum is a bit larger than a man's and apparently does a better job in connecting the two hemispheres. One hypothesis derived from this difference is that women will tend to have a better connection between their verbal skills and their emotions, and that men will tend to be slower in processing emotions on a verbal level. Men are not incapable of doing this; it just takes more time, and they may find it easier to use other non-verbal mechanisms to relieve their emotions.

So far we have determined that the masculine is interested in the future, outcomes, product, efficiency, and goals. He will be less likely to want to put feelings into words, more likely to prefer a quiet path to heal, and less likely to have an abundance of tears. Any attempt to support someone with a strong masculine will need to take these things into account. An instructive example might be found in the history of child therapy. Traditional therapy was found not to be particularly effective with young children. When efforts were made to create a type of therapy that would fit with the clients being supported, play therapy was born. While at play, children feel comfortable, and when they feel comfortable they are much more likely to be in a position to be and feel supported. Likewise, to be supportive to men we should focus on the unique needs and qualities of the masculine.

A good example of the impact of masculine/feminine differences in providing support is how my children learned to ride bicycles. When my firstborn learned to ride, she was happy to have me around her, to keep a hand on the bike, to offer encouragement, and to run along steadying the bike as she rode. When she would crash, she was very happy to have me come up to her, to touch her, to ask if she was okay, and actively console her. So when my son learned to ride I thought I knew exactly how to be most helpful to him. Boy was I in for a surprise! He did not want me to be near him, didn't want me to even look like I was helping, didn't want me to say anything "supportive," and on and on. He wanted to do it himself! I was slow to pick up on this, and continued trying to apply what I had learned from my daughter. Ha! When he crashed, the last thing he wanted was for me to come over and make a big deal out of things. He wanted to get back up and try it again. When I tried to practice my version of helping, he wouldn't say anything but would motion for me to go away! I learned. I also learned that what he did want from me was my presence and my attention. He wanted to be seen, and he wanted the safety of having me present. That was what helped him feel safe, not a great outward show of emotion pointed in his direction.

This example is not meant to be proof of gender differences in children and the way they accept or respond to offers of support. It is, however, meant to be an example of how two children had very different paths, with each needing something very different. It could very well have been the other way around, with my daughter preferring the "hands off" treatment. It doesn't matter which child preferred which mode of support; the important thing is that we all have a different path to seeking solace. As professionals, we need to be aware of this and seek each person's unique way of healing.

Why did my daughter choose one path and my son another? Anthropologists tell us that the first step in any sort of healing is what they call "containment." By containment, they mean safety. My daughter sought out a manner of consolation that felt "safe" to her, as did my son. The first step to any healing is always based on this idea of safety. It bears repeating that we tend not to heal in foxholes under enemy fire, but in places where we feel safe and comfortable. Knowing a person's place of comfort and safety is a good first step in knowing how they will feel supported.

In learning to ride a bicycle my daughter was more in line with Tannen's keyword of intimacy, the concept that she has linked with the feminine. She feels that women in general and those with a preponderance of feminine traits will likely see the world through the primary lens of intimacy. Someone with a preponderance of the feminine energy would be more likely to want support that honored her interest and sense of safety around issues of intimacy. By touching her, asking if she was okay, steadying the bike, and offering support, my daughter felt comfortable. These things harmonized with her keyword of intimacy. By supporting her in this way, I was both giving her support and honoring her path of wanting to feel close and intimate with others. It was a good fit.

My son, on the other hand, does not tend to have a primary keyword of intimacy. He is more in line with the keyword of independence that Tannen ascribes to the masculine. Those with this keyword will tend to see the world in a hierarchical manner and will ask the question, "Who is governing whom?" In other words, who is in charge and where am I on this hierarchy? Tannen feels that it is the masculine nature to see the world through the primary lens of independence. Thus, males tend to be sensitive to situations where their independence is called into question. By allowing my son his space, I was honoring his need for independence and at the same time offering support in a way that was comfortable for him to accept—giving him my attention, my gaze, and my presence. My son felt supported by "being seen" and having my undivided attention as long as it didn't embarrass him in the presence of his own hierarchical group of friends (real or imagined).

With a clear idea of the differences between the masculine and feminine energies, we can begin to ask what specific approaches will honor these differences and be most supportive of men who are healing from loss. The following suggestions do not represent an inclusive or exhaustive list, of course, but are simply some avenues of support that I have found to be particularly effective in helping men.

COMMUNICATION

In talking with men who are healing it is helpful to keep the hierarchical ideas in mind. One example of this is not to ask "How are you feeling?" This question exposes the weakness of the masculine side by asking a man to put feelings immediately into words. Asking instead "What is the toughest thing about this?" is a much better approach. This question still asks about the person's status but in a way that is much more hierarchically friendly. It also honors the person by implying that his situation is difficult.

Another example of this type of approach is the hi-low game. It is a tradition in our house to play hi-low at the dinner table. Hi-low is a game that simply poses the question: What was the worst thing that happened to you today, and what was the best thing that happened? This is a great exercise for young boys. It harmonizes with their hierarchical view and gives them practice in connecting to their personal story. Of course the adults play too, and in this way each person gets to encapsulate his or her day in telling the high and low experiences.

I have found also that men tend to prefer to talk about their grief after they feel they have some dominion over it. Women usually display the opposite tendency, preferring to talk about it in order to obtain some dominion over it. Considering this, it is important to allow men to choose the time when they feel ready to talk about their loss.

SHARED ACTIVITIES

I am often asked whether organizations should run support groups for men. The answer, of course, is that it's good to run support groups because there are men and women who can benefit from this sort of help. But people who have a healthy dose of the masculine may need something a little different from the usual group setup. Those with a strong masculine side often respond better to shared goals and activities that help them connect with the loss. For example, one hospice offered a fishing trip for all of the men whose wives had died the previous year. They provided a charter boat and fishing gear, and told the men that the trip was meant to honor their wives and their loss. The men would spend the day fishing, and in doing so would fish shoulder-to-shoulder with other men who had experienced a similar loss. By the end of the day, these men walked off in pairs and trios, having bonded together in a shared experience that was focused not on their loss, but on fishing.

A shared activity that has a goal has been used for years by men in supporting their sons. When there is a bad time, the father takes the son on a trip or excursion, plays a game, or simply goes out to get a snack. In this way, the activity becomes the foreground, and the giving and getting support becomes the background. Both father and son are more comfortable with this arrangement. They feel more at home sharing an activity that has some goal or outcome that has a beginning and an end. Younger men have traditionally benefited from the older man's empathy and love that is intuitively offered via a shared activity.

One man I know was presented with a situation where his son, who had made some bad decisions about drugs, was in dire need of support. The man suggested that he and his son climb the local mountain. It was not a climb that needed lots of equipment, but a half-day hike up steep hills with the bonus of beautiful scenery from the top. As he and his son climbed, they were able to connect with the issues the son was facing. The climbing took center stage yet allowed them to discuss their issues as they worked toward the top. The goal was to climb the mountain, and as they worked on that goal together they were able to connect and discuss the issues around the son's crisis.

Unfortunately, our culture has eliminated most of the shared activities that men traditionally used to connect with their pain following a death. Activities like building the casket, digging the grave, and transporting the body to the cemetery have all been subcontracted out to professionals. With the exception of giving the eulogy or serving as a pallbearer, the men in our culture have "nothing to do" following a death. There is a great deal of evidence in the literature suggesting that men of other cultures tend to rely on activities following a death in order to connect with their pain. The majority of tribal people give men a task—usually a shared activity that is goal-directed—after a death. Among the Ylongu tribe of Australia, the men sing; in Africa, the Dagura men dance, and some tribes drum continuously for several days to inform other tribes in the region of the death. By performing the task, the men get the opportunity to experience their pain and to honor the person who has died.

These tribal customs provide an important clue in helping us understand what to do for men following a death: give them something to do that will honor the person who died. After my father's death, my brother and I decided to build a wooden container for his ashes. Over the course of the week of the funeral, other men who came to visit our family would join us in Dad's workshop in the garage. As we shared the task of designing and constructing the box, we also shared tears and laughter, telling stories about the father and friend each of us had lost. The activity of making the box served as a "hook" or focal point for our pain, and the workshop functioned as a "container," a safe place where we could connect to our pain and tears. We men felt a sense of safety as we worked shoulder-to-shoulder, and thus were able to grieve in a way that would not have been possible had we been sitting in a circle facing one another. One of the reasons men tend to have an easier time in connecting their grief with action is because they have a harder time connecting their emotions with words. The task of building a box for my father's ashes provided us with a shared activity, a common goal, and a safe place to release our grief.

HUMOR

It may surprise some to learn that the masculine side tends to use humor as a means of support. I have seen men use humor as a way to be able to touch the subject of a loss without becoming overwhelmed by it. It is a way to detach a bit.

For those who are more used to the feminine path, humor in the face of death or tragedy may seem in bad taste. But usually the humor is simply being used as a means to detach and acknowledge. There are many things for which we need support that are simply too big to accept and digest in one bite. Humor is a way to engage a small piece of the pain at a time and to be able to detach from it through the healing power of laughter.

My personal example of this kind of support through humor comes from a group of men I belong to who have been meeting, and supporting one another, for years. One of the group once had a teacher who had a standard response he gave to anyone who was going through a rough time. The teacher, who was Asian, would say "It's a not so bad" in a singsong, but caring manner. When we heard of some of the dire situations of the people to whom the teacher had said this, it was hilarious to think of anyone saying such a thing. But the remarkable thing is that the teacher almost always received a positive reaction to his phrase. People really appreciated his words. The phrase has become a staple of our group, and we use it in our mutual support. Hearing "It's a not so bad" always brings a smile, and the entire group enjoys a good laugh as we acknowledge the difficulty of life and begin to detach a bit through our laughter.

GIVING THROUGH DOING

We have seen how the masculine values activity and product; we also can use these as a means to offer support. When considering how to support someone with strong masculine traits, you might want to think about doing something for them or doing something in honor of the reason for their loss. Ideas include starting a scholarship fund, donating money to a cause in honor of the loss, building a memorial, etc. A woman I know helped a male friend construct a Japanese garden in memory of his son who had died suddenly while climbing a mountain in Argentina. Together they cleared an area in the man's back yard, hauled in and spread decorative gravel, and set a stone statue. As they worked, the man was able to share some of his grief. Since activity is such a vital mechanism for those with a strong masculine to use to connect with their pain, it is no surprise that it also serves as a means for anyone to be able to offer support.

CONSULTATION VERSUS CONSOLATION

Those with a preponderance of the masculine energy usually come into therapy seeking a consultation. That is, the person is looking for help in finding the way through a difficult situation. I have noticed in my practice that a woman will come into treatment seeking a regular weekly time to meet. She generally feels comfortable with this, and it suits her nature. Men, on the other hand, seem to prefer to come in for short consultations. I have learned that a man will come in for two to four sessions, and then go back out into his world and work on his issues. Six months later he may come back for another few sessions, and then it's back out into his world again. The man seems to be more comfortable seeking a consultation from an expert rather than setting a time for support. At one time I used to encourage men to come in on a weekly basis, but I generally don't anymore. If the man feels that it is best for him to have weekly times I am pleased to comply, but first I try to find out what he wants and go with that.

RESPECT

An important element in supporting the masculine side is understanding the impact of respect. Why is this so? Respect is the currency of the masculine. When you live in a world based on hierarchy and who is governing whom, you are sensitized to issues of respect. Webster's tells us that respect means "To consider deserving of high regard." In the hierarchy, men try to gather respect, to be considered deserving of high regard by their peers. What I have noticed in groups of men is that feeling respected seems to be a prerequisite for opening up about problems. In some ways this is a parallel to the woman's situation of needing to feel close to someone before opening up emotionally. When a man feels he is in the company of others who truly respect him, he is more likely to let his guard down and be open about his situation. He no longer feels a need to posture or maintain an image in order to be respected, and he can relax a bit and open up. In the group of men I have been meeting with for many years, we realized that the depth of our discussions and our closeness was related to our sense of being respected by each other. When we feel respected, we tend to automatically relax and take on a more open stance. I have seen instances of a wife letting her husband know how much he is respected and being surprised by his response of talking about a difficult personal issue.

So how can we show respect in trying to be supportive to men? One way is to respect a man's emotional space—respect his need to emote, or more importantly, his need not to emote. Offer your attention and support, but allow him to refuse it, to avoid the topic if he wishes. A good guide might be to treat him with the idea of service in your mind: How can you be of service to him? When we are serving others we are usually treating them as if they are one-up on the "hierarchy." This can be contrasted with the concept of "helping," which has an implication of treating them as if they are one-down on the hierarchy. Helping implies someone needs help! When you live in a world that values independence, you try to avoid appearing as though you need help. The idea of being served is more harmonious and welcome to a strong masculine type. Another guide might be to think of the Japanese culture and their emphasis on respect and "saving face."

SUMMARY

Each person has a unique pathway of healing and a unique pathway of support. In trying to figure out how we can best support someone, it is important to consider the person's blend of masculine and feminine energies. As we have seen, the masculine side values independence and sees the world through a lens of who is governing whom. This hierarchical worldview lends itself to an interest in output, product, efficiency, and goals. There is nothing wrong with this viewpoint; it is simply different from the feminine perspective of intimacy and sharing.

These two energies are not black and white, but blend into a finely shaded gray. Knowing someone's natural balance of masculine and feminine—his or her shade of gray—gives us valuable information as to what kind of support will be most helpful. Anyone whose balance is masculine will naturally have a different path in finding healing and support than someone whose balance is feminine. For those with a preponderance of the masculine, the most effective and welcome support will be that which aligns with the value of independence and a hierarchical worldview. Shared activities, honoring and acknowledging through doing, preferring the future as a ground for healing, and being more quiet are a few of the approaches that we have discussed.

As we progress through the new century it is increasingly important that we do so with a widening understanding of our individual differences and a tolerance for those who differ from our own ways. Understanding our differences on the scale of masculine and feminine is an important step in that direction.

My thanks to Helen Wadsworth, James Jones, Darbie Golden, Miles Goldstein, Michael Abrahams, and Jon Ladd for their wisdom and input in creating this chapter. Additional thanks to the good teachers of Webhealing.com and GriefCeu.com

REFERENCE

1. T. R. Golden, *Swallowed by a Snake: The Gift of the Masculine Side of Healing,* Golden Healing Publishing, Gaithersberg, Maryland, 2000.

CHAPTER 8

Social Support for Adults with Developmental Disabilities

Marie Antoinette Parisio

My interest in the subject of persons with developmental disabilities and grief was first aroused after hearing the deep pain of guilt, rejection, anger, and frustration in many of my friends in L'Arche and as well as in Faith and Light, which are international communities where adults with developmental disabilities are at the core.

Adults with developmental disabilities because of their intellectual impairment have often been denied the right to grieve: "he does not understand," "do not tell her, it will upset her too much," "let us pretend that nothing happened so that she does not get too sad." They have most surely been disenfranchised by society. However, their loss tells more about us than about them. When accepted by their parents, adults with developmental challenges do have a very strong attachment to them; moreover, they depend on them for many aspects of their life: identity, self-esteem, and security. Like many of us, if grief work is not done after a significant loss, people with developmental challenges will demonstrate mal-adapted behaviors or behavior problems because of the difficulty of integrating the loss. At times, the pain experienced after the loss of a loved one, a parent, a caregiver, or a friend seems disproportionate to the attachment that person had to the deceased. Furthermore, the pain becomes complicated when the attachment did not take place or feelings of ambivalence were experienced by the mourner in his/her relationship with the deceased.

In this chapter I will talk about losses by death; however, I am well aware that very often persons with developmental challenges suffer multiple losses—home, family, and security—with the passing of a parent or main caregiver.

I believe that before trying to help a specific population with grief, one needs to understand what grief is and how bereavement and mourning are understood according to Worden, Rando, and other specialists in the field. Luchterhand and

Murphy, in their book *Helping Adults with Mental Retardation Grieve a Death Loss,* help us recognize the fact that "adults with developmental disabilities are more similar than different in the feelings and other reactions they experience as they grieve and adapt to loss" [1, p. 1]. The difficulties for the bereaved population of adults with developmental disabilities may come from their cognitive difficulties [1, p. 16], or the expression of their emotions which is going to translate the true feeling [1, p. 18]. More often than not, it is a behavior which is going to translate their true feelings [1, p. 16]. Moreover, society around them does not treat them in the same way it does other members; either they are perceived as needing to be protected from harsh reality or they are not allowed to talk about the fact. Persons with developmental disabilities make up a segment of society that has experienced multiple losses over time [1, p. 24] and that lacks social support in general and even more so at times of death [1, p. 24]. If the person who died is the main care giver, the sense of insecurity experienced by the bereaved might be overwhelming [1, p. 25] and brings with it the prospect of a very uncertain sense of the future [1, p. 25]. In many cases, family members and/ or staff are needed to act as reporters or interpreters [1, p. 22]. "Two important procedures are to tell the person with mental retardation about the deaths of people close to them and allow them time to grieve" [1, p. 27]. Although for most of us it might seem a very basic right, the author reminds us that, unfortunately, it is not always the case for the developmentally challenged segment of society.

In this chapter I would like to offer some reflections and thoughts on delivering care to adults who have developmental challenges. With Murphy and Luchterhand, I agree that adults with developmental challenges are more similar than different from us in their grief process work. A few years ago, I worked on a *Grief Work Support Group Manual* as an exercise for the certificate in thanatology. I believe group support can be a tool to offer support to adults with developmental challenges, a group of people who meet together regularly to help one another by sharing what they carry and what they have learned out of their common experience. "The need is enormous for there are many people with developmental disabilities who do not have even a small group of committed friends and neighbors who will help them generate and realize their dreams" (Nathan Ball, Director and Community Leader [2]), or help them through the process of grief work. The group would also include two skilled facilitators and a veteran with developmental challenges who had experienced the same loss and had worked it through, and this to reinforce the modeling and exert her/his caring skills. "We believe that powerlessness is dispelled when people reach out and form new relationships in response to a need" [2]. By forming a group for this vulnerable population I believe it would

- initiate the grief work;
- identify and express feelings and thoughts in a safe, supportive, and nonjudgmental space;

- also acknowledge the right to grieve of all human beings, each being unique;
- begin the healing process and allow growth;
- offer support and permission to grieve: "you hurt and I hurt too when I lost someone I loved." It is a normal and universal pain. We can help each other by sharing that pain, in trying to understand the acting-out or maladaptive behaviors;
- empower the person; and
- give an opportunity to socialize with others who went through a similar experience.

To be a member of such a group one needs to have

- experienced the same kind of loss through death;
- come freely;
- gone through a pre-screening to insure that the group is appropriate; and
- received the consent of a competent guardian or doctor in case the need arises to get professional help during the process.

According to Kaufman:

> mentally retarded people have strong and obsessive characteristics to their processing of thoughts and feelings troubling thoughts and affective disturbances tend to be especially persistent. We sometimes see a repetition of the same thought or feeling over and over, suggesting the person is having difficulty in acknowledging and integrating the death [cited in 3, p. 31].

If the mourner is stuck in a complicated place or enters into a crisis triggered by the grief work, he or she may need to be referred to his/her doctor for extra and appropriate support and/or treatment besides the group.

The place where the group meets will be as neutral as possible, not a group home or in a building that carries the stigma of impaired functioning individuals; rather a warm, homey, and cozy place easily accessible by bus (many people with developmental disabilities depend on the bus and have limited budgets to cover taxi expenses). People from the group will gather in a circle, on comfortable chairs, all at the same level for eye contact to ensure better communication.

Meetings could take place once a week for 12 weeks. Mourning is a process, not an event. Friends with developmental disabilities process information slowly. Because grief work is hard work and the capacity for concentration is limited, one session cannot exceed two hours including the break for socialization and friendship. The meeting has to stay short.

The role of the facilitators is:

- to create a safe environment;
- to facilitate the meeting;
- to see the bereaved as active participants;
- to explain the process;

- to listen well to words as well as to body language;
- to model the sharing;
- to manage time so that every member gets enough time;
- to initiate the activities;
- to redirect and refocus the group if needed; and
- to create conditions that allow the bereaved to start the work of mourning.

Two complementary facilitators who know the population of adults with developmental disabilities well and know how to relate to them are essential. If a crisis arises and a member needs one-on-one, the required help will be possible. No professionals will be directly involved in the meetings; however, they will be available for back-up in case the need arises as well as for referrals or for education at times.

The screening before the group starts will serve three purposes:

1. to help the facilitators feel if there is cohesion in the group, if it is the right group for the mourner (one on one counseling might be needed before one can join the group);
2. to determine the level of communication, both verbal and non verbal; and
3. to gather a minimum of information about the person and the death he or she experienced (sickness, accident, old age . . .).

I believe screening is crucial. There should be about five or six members for the group. Too large a group would be hard to lead and make it difficult to accomplish real goals. A group of three or four would be too small to allow enough sharing of experiences and to keep on finding support in the group.

To operate properly, ground rules are necessary. Examples could include the following:

- We will start and end on time.
- We will keep the confidentiality of the group.
- We will wish everyone goodwill.
- We will be present at every meeting.
- We will listen without judging.
- We will not interrupt.
- We will not give advice.
- What we feel is our reality. There are no right or wrong feelings, thoughts. Everyone is unique.
- It is all right not to talk if we do not want to.
- We will try to stay on a topic.
- It is okay to cry.

The grief work will be spread out over the 12 weeks.

- week one: representation of death
- week two: the challenge of being left behind after a death

- week three: the loss of support and security
- week four: remembering who the person was for me
- week five: remembering who I was for the person who died
- week six: how to be safe again?
- week seven: letting go
- week eight: exploring the feelings of being abandoned
- week nine: self-worth and self-esteem
- week ten: self-empowerment
- week eleven: from crisis to healing and growth
- week twelve: celebration

Each week, the gathering will start at 7 P.M.; however, the team will be there at 6 P.M. to set up the room and be there to welcome people when they arrive.

Every week will follow a certain routine: sit in a circle, welcome, light the candle, the pledge (which I will introduce in the next paragraph), grief work, distribution of homework for the next session, and a closing ritual (blowing out the candle being the last step).

During the first week, the pledge is introduced: I will be here every week and on time, I will not reveal any information from the group to another group or place. I wish goodwill to everyone.

The ground rules will also be introduced.

The methodology of the first night includes making something together and telling a story. The aim for that particular and key night is to get to know each other in a nonthreatening way and to build support and trust. Each participant will draw or paint or glue elements he or she has chosen on the small square of felt (s)he received in response to the question: "What is death for you?" This work will be done while listening to quiet music. Then each mourner will show and explain his/her piece of art (color used, material, representation . . .). At the end, the members of the group will assemble all the squares to make a quilt that will be used along with the candle as a centerpiece for the weekly gathering. It is a visual and tactile symbol of the group and its focus. Later on, after the break, during which we have soft drinks and goodies, people will listen to a story entitled *Lifetimes* by Bryan Mellanie and Robert Ingpen [4]. Then they will be invited to bring pictures of the person they lost the following week, and one volunteer will be asked to bring cookies for the next session. The checkout time will be important for the facilitators to sense how it went and if it was a good start for the group.

The second week will follow the same pattern. The atmosphere will be created before the group starts, but the candle will signal the beginning of the gathering. The pledge will be reintroduced and modeled before everyone checks in with: name, how you feel tonight, and how your week was. Another story will be read: *When my Mommy Died* by Janice Hammond [5]. I am aware that this is a children's story and I certainly do not want to use it to baby the adults I work with. I only recognize that it is difficult to find books that are appropriate for the group I work with, i.e., both simple enough and containing adult photos. I also recognize that faced with the death of my parents, it is the child within me who cried for help.

Some children's books are beautiful and address the topic of death and grief quite well. Furthermore the people I work with are cognitively impaired and do not function well in the abstract. The book allows the participants to identify with a vulnerable child who lost his mother and gives them permission to experience genuine feelings and the normality of these feelings. There is no right, no wrong.

The second night is still a place where we aim at building trust and support. Also, we are going to introduce the person who died in our life with the pictures we brought. Each person can have five to seven minutes if needed. The facilitator will keep track of time and help the group stay on topic. Participants will share their feelings, their fears, their losses, and describe what life has been since the loss.

At the end of the second meeting, it is extremely important to check out and tell how you feel. After holding hands, we will blow out the candle.

The third week the same will happen, we will start on time at seven, with everything prepared ahead of time. To help people remember names we will play a game before the pledge; then we will answer the questions: How has the week been? How do you feel right now? The work is going to recall events, vacations, trips, weddings in the family where I and the person I mourn were together, recall and release emotions: It is ok to cry, acknowledge the role the person was playing in my life, name it: support, parent as anchors of one's life. Again go back to the photo you brought, in dyads talk about the person for five minutes then share with the full group. After a break, draw a picture of you and the person you miss in your journal, while listening to harp music. The homework will be a volunteer for cookies, and for all to bring a keepsake which is precious to you and which is associated with, or represents the person who died. At the end share around the circle how you feel now and about tonight, hold hands, and blow out the candle.

Week four will start on time, with a warm welcome for all. After the candle is lit, we will recall the focus of the group and the names and pledge before checking in with where you are now, holding the photo of your beloved one who died. All the participants have the same experience in common, and it strengthens them to share it.

A ritual of lighting a small candle beside the photograph on the common quilt will take place, and people will be INVITED again to share, under the guidance of the facilitator. Do you remember how old you were when it happened? How did she/he die? Where were you? Were you told? Who told you? Did you have a chance to say goodbye?

After that intense sharing, we will have a 10-minute break. When we return, we will show the keepsake we brought and express why we chose it and what it represents for us. It is crucial for the facilitators to listen well to verbal and body language and to facilitate the expressions of feelings. For homework for next week, in your journal draw a picture of the person you talked about tonight or cut out a picture that represents her/him. Before leaving the group, while listening to music, each person is reminded that she/he is beautiful, loveable, that he/she has a great deal to offer to others. Holding hands, we conclude and blow out the candle.

Week five will shape itself on the same pattern as the previous one. The topic is on the mourner/participant. Who was I in the person's life that died? Before that, we will have the welcome, the lightening of the candle, the names and pledge, the check in: how are you feeling now?

Looking at our journal, what we drew or the picture we cut out and glued in our journal, we will talk about our attachment to the person. We will share some happy times and/or some hard times in our relationship with the person who has died. Each participant will have five to seven minutes to talk about how (s)he felt about the person. Did (s)he feel loved, rejected? Did (s)he love the person? Did (s)he hate him or her? Why? All feelings are acceptable. No judgments can take place; there is no right, no wrong. The role of the facilitator is to invite the expression of feelings, to get in touch with emotions, to stay on topic and to listen well. After the sharing time, people can write a note, a letter, or draw a picture to give or ask for forgiveness from the dead person and place it by the photo.

After the break we will talk about the wake, the funeral. Was I able to go? Who was there with me? If I did not go, why didn't I? How did I feel about it?

The evening will conclude on an exercise of visualization again while listening to music: you are beautiful, you are loveable, and you have a lot to offer to others. The homework for next week aside from the volunteer for cookies, will be to draw how I feel when I think of the person or to use some stickers available to choose from: happy, tense, sick, guilty. After holding hands, we will blow out the candle.

Week six will be about how to be safe again. At 7 P.M. the group will meet. The routine is well established now: on time, in a circle, light the candle, pledge, check in.

A text will be read from the book *Healing the Bereaved Child* [3, p. 194] while we have our photos on the quilt, our journals open in front of us:

We remember them
In the rising of the sun and its going down,
we remember them;

In the blowing of the wind and in the chill of winter,
we remember them;

In the warmth of the sun and the peace of the summer,
we remember them;

In the rustling of the leaves and the beauty of autumn,
we remember them;

In the beginning of the year and when it ends,
we remember them;

When we are weary and in need of strength,
we remember them;

When we are lost and sick at heart,
we remember them;

When we have joys we yearn to share,
we remember them;

So long as we live, they too shall live,
for they are now part of us,
as we remember them.

We will share the feelings we carry and we will be reminded that it is ok to feel what we feel. We will gain strength from the group in sharing information and in being listened to and understood, not judged. The exercise is to help us let go of the person who died and gradually move to new security, supports. If needed, we will again talk about the death, the illness, or the circumstances prior to the death and/or the funeral. The poem will be read another time by two alternating readers in a soft voice, as peaceful musical is played in the background. After the break, people will make a frame with material that is available and frame the picture they have journeyed with. The homework will be to place it on a wall in a place at home if it is what they desire. The frame making will help integrate the loss. The poem will be given to each participant to decorate and put in his or her own journal. Before finishing the group will gather and refocus, then check in and tell how you feel about tonight, hold hands and blow out the candle.

Week seven's focus is on letting go. Same routine as usual to begin. The aim of tonight is to say goodbye to the person who has died and to release emotions and share a common experience. With soft background music, members of the group will be asked to close their eyes; we will say goodbye to the person and accept the fact that he/she will not come back. We admit that their loss still hurts a lot, that we are on a journey of healing, and that we are not alone anymore.

After a 10-minute break, each participant will choose a heart-shaped balloon, inflate it and then as a group we will go to the park and release them. It is our way to express our last goodbye. In your journal for next week draw your hands as well as your loving heart and the heart balloon you have let go today.

Gathering around the candle, we will sing the first two verses of Amazing Grace, before checking out: how was tonight's experience? We will hold hands and blow out the candle.

Week eight will be the exploration of feelings. The introduction to the evening is now routine, after checking in we will answer the question: tell us about something you recalled during the week that kept the person who died alive for you (a word, a song, a flower, a smell, a taste . . .).

This particular night people will work in pairs. They will explore the challenges of losses discussing different topics. The facilitator proposes a question, answers to which the pair shares; then another question is offered:

what bothers you most about having lost that significant person?
share a difficult experience that you had recently
what difficulty are you having with friends?
share a time where you have been angry when someone hurt your feelings
share a time where you have felt afraid
share a time when you felt lonely
how do you show anger?
how do you express that you are afraid?
how do you express that you are lonely?

After all groups have gone through all the questions, they return to the circle to share some information with the group. The role of the facilitator is to affirm the participants, help them realize their common experience by listening to each other. After the break, go through magazines, choose pictures which talk to you, tear them out in silence, glue them into your journal, look at them, discuss why you like them. Do you want to share your collage with the group? Are you open to the group input? In this exercise, again, the role of the facilitator is to affirm the participants: it is ok to be afraid, to be lonely, to be sad, to be angry.

Homework for next week: aside from a volunteer for cookies, you can add to your collage. Pamper yourself and remember that you are loveable, kind, and loving. You have a lot to offer to the world. After the check out, blow out the candle.

The ninth week will explore self-worth and self-esteem. Fabric, markers, glue . . . will be available. The question after the check in will be: share what made you happy this past week.

The aim of this evening is to acknowledge what we have learned out of crisis, recognize that we have helped and supported each other, recognize that we can be life-givers to others, and that there is hope and life in our existence.

Each participant will choose two squares of material, a larger one of cotton and a smaller one of felt. On the felt one, represent what life is for you. You can draw, paint, or glue elements. You create something beautiful while listening to music.

After the break, glue your art onto the cotton cloth, stop and look at it, then show it to the group and share your creation with the group, welcome input and observations from the group, take it home and hang it in a private space.

The homework will be to find a meaningful place for your artwork. Think about what you would like to do for the last meeting. By asking for ideas, you help people realize that the group will stop in a couple of weeks.

Week ten will be about self-empowerment. The check in will be followed by the questions: How was the week? Did you show your artwork to someone? Where did you display it? Would you like to show your collage if you added something to it? And how are you feeling now?

The facilitator will outline what grief work has been done so far and introduce the coming end of the group: Is it another loss? Acknowledge the pain; look at the future; and introduce the moving-on.

During a few minutes of quiet time while listening to music, reflect on what you have learned about yourself, about others, about the grief process, about your loss.

Get back together for group sharing.

Then, in pairs, share how you feel about the ending of the group in two weeks time

- in your journal draw a face expressing how you feel
- share briefly with the group.

After the break, get together for relaxation with slides and music. Picture yourself by a lake looking at the sky, and listen: "I am loveable, kind, and loving. I deserve the best in life. I have a lot to offer. I love the world, the world loves me. I am willing to be happy. I do not have to please others. The world is a good place to be."

Homework for next week: aside from the goodies, think of which activities feed your spirit and make you happy (swimming, cooking, walking, drawing, gardening . . .).

Draw the activities in your journal and think about our last meeting. What do we want to do? We conclude with our now well-established ritual: check out, hold hands, and blow out the candle.

Week eleven is from crisis to healing and growth. The team will have the room ready, the material in place before the participants arrive. The goal is to recognize that we have learned something from crisis, and to empower ourselves and to trust in the future. It is also to understand and appreciate who we are, and acknowledge that we are in a process of growth, of healing, of transformation. It is also to affirm each other's gifts. New life is born.

We will start with the lighting of the candle, the check in, and talk about the ending of the group, the pledge.

The first activity is to paint our hand in our journal. While it dries, we will share on what we have learned during these 10 weeks, how I am transformed. Then we will look at the future, how am I going to keep healing and growing on my own, with my family members, with my friends?

We will go back to our journals. Everyone will write or draw beside the hand what gift the person brought to the group and (s)he will carry with him/her to the world. We write or draw in every journal. An exercise of visualization will follow: close our eyes, picture ourselves happy with family members at a family reunion, when we visit. Visualize ourselves happy and making new friends out there in the world, outside of our group.

For homework reflect on how you will continue the group when the group is over. Also take the evaluation sheet home (it is in the annex of this chapter) and fill it out yourself or with the help of someone you trust.

After the break, discussion of the celebration on the last day next week, of who brings what for the potluck, exchange of addresses or phone numbers, games, music, jokes. . . .

Hold hands and choose a pot of flowers to take home and care for. These daffodils or tulips are a sign of spring, of new life, of new beginning. Check out and blow out of the candle.

Week twelve is the celebration. An inviting, warm atmosphere is created with flowers, candles, and tablecloths. First we will conduct the oral evaluation of the group. Then the potluck starts the celebration. After the time of festival, the group gathers in a circle and to live the ritual of closure of the group and of being sent to her/his personal path. Each participant receives a candle that will be lightened from the group candle. (S)he will carry it home as a reminder of the energy of the group.

The homework will be in the journal:

- take good care of yourself;
- keep working on your journal, write or draw your feelings. It is your personal and sacred book.

The check out will include a comparison of my feelings today and when we met the first time. The facilitator will blow out the group candle, and each participant will leave the room with his/her personal candle lit, then will blow it out.

In this chapter I have focused on grief work in the context of a support group for adults with developmental disabilities; some of the ideas I have used come from my experiences with these adults, my readings, conversations with grief counselors, or family members.

In their book *Helping Adults with Mental Retardation Grieve a Death Loss*, Luchterhand and Murphy (chapter 4) gather a menu of more than one hundred strategies to assist this particular population deal with grief. Some are creative, physical, involve music, outdoors, nature, rituals, and traditions (religious or spiritual).

The role of the group support or of all the strategies is to support the person in his/her grief work and allow her/him to accomplish the four tasks Worden describes:

1. to accept the reality of the loss;
2. to feel the pain of the loss;
3. to adjust to a world where the deceased is missing; and
4. to withdraw emotional energy and reinvest in the world with a new energy.

Adults with developmental disabilities, like all of us, have the right to know about the losses and to be offered the space and means to grieve. The coping techniques are no different for them than they are for anyone. In fact, in my experience, I have seen adults with developmental disabilities who have had a chance to grieve become a healing presence for others in grief. To offer that presence they need to receive real support when they need it.

EVALUATION SHEET

Complete the following questionnaire to assist in future planning. If needed, get the help of someone you trust to help you.

	Poor	Fair	Good	Excellent
1-Length of the course				
2-Size of the group				
3-Meeting time				
4-Meeting place				
5-Value of the group to you				
6-Use of time				
7-Method of sharing				
8-Choice of topics				
9-Opportunity for participation				
10-Met your personal needs				

Was the information useful to you?

What else would you like to see covered?

How can we better meet your needs?

Signature:______________________________

REFERENCES

1. C. Luchterhand and N. Murphy, *Helping Adults with Mental Retardation Grieve a Death Loss,* Accelerated Development, Philadelphia, Pennsylvania, 1998.
2. N. Ball, *Daybreak Newsbreak,* Toronto, Winter 1997.
3. A. D. Wolfelt, *Healing the Bereaved Child,* Companion Press, Fort Collins, Colorado, 1996.
4. M. Bryan and R. Ingpen, *Lifetimes,* Bantam Books, Toronto, 1983.
5. J. Hammond, *When My Mommy Died,* Cranbrook, Flint, Michigan, 1980.

CHAPTER 9

Social Support in Suicide Prevention

Antoon A. Leenaars, David Lester, and Susanne Wenckstern

Childhood and adolescent problems in adjustment have been an increasing concern since the last century. In 1910, Sigmund Freud and his colleagues identified numerous problems in youth, highlighting suicide [1]. By the 1960s, up to 30 percent of youth in developed countries were identified as displaying some maladjustment [2], with current rates being even higher, and about 1–3 percent of youths' psychopathology being labeled as being serious [3]. Schools are natural environments to provide social support for these problems through prevention programs.

Young people in most parts of the world attend school. Schools are institutions designed to socially support a child and adolescent's development and to address the problems of children and youth. There are numerous programs to address these problems, e.g., health, sex and AIDS education, suicide prevention, drinking and driving, substance abuse, and violence programs. There are also programs to address academic needs and to promote personal and social growth. There are numerous reasons for these efforts. The primary one is that health care systems alone cannot meet all the needs of youth [3].

Suicide is an important mental health and public health problem worldwide [4]. Adolescents and even children commit suicide [5]. An even greater number of youth attempt or seriously think about suicide as the solution to their life's difficulties [6, 7]. As was stated at the turn of the last century [1], schools and communities must respond [8].

What can we do? What can teachers, other school staff, and community personnel in social support systems do? What can we do to be supportive in schools? In most cases, something can be done to save a young life. Shneidman has made a very important observation regarding this concern, namely that about 80 percent of suicides provide clues to their imminent suicide [9]. Regrettably, the clues to suicide are usually not responded to before the act, and sometimes they are not even seen or heard. It follows that education about the facts of suicide would help us to prevent suicide. Most people would agree that the best prevention is primary prevention (preventing suicide from ever occurring), and primary prevention involves, among other things, education. It is important to teach which clues should be looked for, what can be done, and what help is available.

School staff are in a unique position to recognize the possibility of suicide and to take preventive action. Teachers and other school staff especially can make a major contribution to saving a life. After a few opening remarks about the rationale for programs in schools of a comprehensive nature, this chapter presents a section on prevention, relating primarily to dissemination of information. As examples of such prevention programs, we outline some common clues to suicide and what to do. The next section reviews the literature, reporting what works. What is sound support in schools?

RATIONALE

The rationale for beginning a suicide prevention program in schools [10] includes the following:

1. The sheer numbers of suicides and suicidal behaviors in youth worldwide.
2. The large number of unhappy—many depressed—youth. Kazdin [11] reported that only 10 to 30 percent of youth needing clinical help, receive that care. It can, thus, be asked: How many suicidal youth are not identified as at risk?
3. There is a possible suggestibility or imitation factor and subsequent contagion. Reflecting on the first documented postvention in schools in the literature, Leenaars [12] noted this fact, something subsequently supported by research [13].
4. Schools are asking for assistance. Thus, it would be wise that the most knowledgeable professionals (educators, social workers, psychologists, etc.) assist.
5. The survivors of suicide are a striking reason. All too many youth in our schools are traumatized by the suicide of their peers [12].

To conclude, there is a rationale for suicide prevention in schools. The important question is not *that* we do it, but *how* teachers and school/community staff can provide social support in schools.

PREVENTION/INTERVENTION/POSTVENTION

The classical approach to the prevention of mental health and public health problems is that of Caplan [14], who differentiated between primary, secondary, and tertiary prevention. The more commonly used concepts today for these three modes of *prevention* are prevention, intervention, and postvention, respectively. Caplan's view still provides the best model for social support for suicide in schools. Briefly, the three modes of a comprehensive response refer to the following:

1. Prevention relates to the principle of good mental hygiene in general. It consists of strategies to ameliorate the conditions that lead to suicide: to do something before the event occurs. Preventing suicide is best accomplished through primary prevention. Prevention is education. Young people (and their gatekeepers) must be educated about suicide. Such education—given that suicide is a multidimensional malaise—is enormously complicated, almost tantamount to preventing human misery.

2. Intervention relates to the treatment and care of a suicidal crisis or suicidal problem. Secondary prevention is doing something during the event. Suicide is an event with biological, psychological, interpersonal, sociocultural, and philosophical/existential aspects. Obviously, suicide is not solely a medical problem, and many people can serve as lifesaving agents. Nonetheless, professionally trained people, psychologists, psychiatrists, social workers, psychiatric nurses, crisis workers, and so on continue to play the primary roles in intervention. Thus, although equally true for postvention, intervention in schools will call for the development of community linkages, a hallmark of a public health response.

3. *Postvention,* a term introduced by Shneidman [see 15], refers to those things done after the event has occurred. Postvention deals with the traumatic after-effects in the survivors of a person who has committed suicide (or in those close to someone who has attempted suicide). It involves offering mental health and public health services to the bereaved survivors. It includes working with all survivors who are in need: children, parents, teachers, etc.

Next, we will outline in more detail some aspects of the first mode of prevention, i.e., primary prevention, which is the focus of our chapter.

PREVENTION: CLUES TO SUICIDE

Effective suicide prevention programs are now found in many schools in the United States, Canada, and a few other countries [16, 17]. They are designed to educate. The main goal of prevention programs is to educate the entire school and community. One begins with the administrators, teachers, and staff (e.g., psychologists, secretaries, bus drivers) and then the students and parents. To be brief, typically after an introduction on the topic (for example, a presentation of national statistics), we have found it most helpful to introduce the audience to two preliminary key words in suicidology: lethality and perturbation (lethality refers to the probability of a person killing him/herself—ranging from low, medium, to high; perturbation refers to how upset, agitated, and so on the person is—also ranging from low, medium, to high). These keys allow one to not only understand but also differentiate the clues (e.g., Is this a low or high-risk situation?). This is followed by facts and myths, as an active participation tool. Next, one outlines the clues to suicide (i.e., previous attempts, verbal statements, cognitive clues, emotional clues, sudden behavioral changes, life-threatening behavior, and suicide notes), followed by the main focus, help seeking. Educational programs for students, teachers, and so on, should stress how to get help. Yet, prevention programs should teach more. Although there is no disagreement that teachers, administrators, and so on should be informed about suicide dynamics and psychopathology (e.g., unbearable pain, depression), there is some controversy about whether students should be informed about psychopathology and suicide risk. We strongly believe that not to discuss this matter is to regress to the simplistic explanation of stress and suicide. Some students were in the past even told, "suicide is normal." Suicide occurs in psychopathology, not normality. Students must be informed about this fact. This is not to say that one outlines in detail the dynamics of suicide to students, only that it is stated in a paragraph or so. Students need to be able to frame (construct) the need to help in the realities of the unbearable pain of suicide. With teachers, counselors, etc., one would be more detailed and one may explicate, for example, the following: definition, concept of death, depression, learning disabilities, physical disabilities and illness, specific environmental precipitating events, and the family system (and the school system). Yet, the main goal of our programs in schools should always be identification and help seeking.

Although we cannot outline here a complete program, we can isolate a few aspects. First, it is important that everyone be aware of the clues that point to potential suicidal behavior. The following list cites a number of important clues that point to suicidal potentiality:

1. Previous Attempts: Although it is obvious that one has to attempt suicide in order to commit it, it is equally clear that the event of attempting suicide need not have death as its objective. It is useful to think of the attempter, sometimes referred to as a parasuicide or as a self-injurer, and the completer as two different parts of overlapping populations: one is a group of those who attempt suicide, a few of whom go on to commit suicide, and the other is a group who commit suicide, a few of whom may have previously attempted to kill themselves. A great deal has to do with the lethality of the action. The ratio between suicide attempts and completions in the general population is about 8 to 1; 1 committed suicide for every 8 attempts. However, in teenagers some studies report a rate of 50 to 1, even 100 to 1. No such data are yet available for children.

A previous attempt is a good clue to the possibility of future attempts, especially if no assistance is obtained after the first attempt, but not all attempters go on to attempt again (or kill themselves). However, all too frequently such behavior is not taken seriously. We recall a very depressed 11-year-old girl who cut her wrists at school. The principal's response was merely, "She is just trying to get attention." What an extreme way to get attention! The girl was moderately lethal and highly perturbed, and required considerable intervention.

2. Verbal Statements: The attitude is often negative toward individuals who make verbal threats of suicide. Suicidal threats are frequently seen as only attempts to get attention. This attitude results in writing-off and ignoring the behavior of a person who is genuinely perturbed and potentially suicidal. Also, it is a well-documented fact that questioning a person about possible suicidal behavior will not increase the chance that they will commit suicide. The important question is, "Why has this person chosen this particular way of getting attention when there are so many other ways?" Examples of direct verbal statements from young people are: "I'm going to kill myself" or "I want to die." More indirect examples are: "I am going to see my (deceased) mother" or "I always knew that I'd die at an early age."

3. Cognitive Clues: The single most common state of mind of a suicidal person is known as constriction. There is tunnel vision, in other words, a narrowing of the mind's eye. There is a narrowing of the range of perceptions, opinions, or options that occur to the person. The person frequently uses words like "only," "always," "never," and "forever." Examples of this in young people are the following: "No one will ever love me. Only Mom loved me"; "John was the only one who loved me"; "My teacher will always be that way"; and "Either I'll kill my brother or myself."

4. Emotional Clues: The child or teenager who is suicidal is often highly perturbed. He/she is disturbed, anxious, and perhaps agitated. Indeed, suicide is not normal; studies show that up to 90 percent are related to psychopathology (mental disorders). Depression is frequently evident, possibly in as many as 60 percent of the cases [18]. Suicidal teenagers are often very angry and hostile and may feel boxed in, rejected, harassed, and unsuccessful. A common emotional state in most suicidal people is hopelessness/helplessness. Hopelessness frequently reveals itself in statements such as: "Nothing will change. It will always be this way." The helplessness can sound like this, "There is nothing I can do. There is nothing my teacher can do."

5. Sudden Behavioral Changes: Changes in behavior may also be predictors of suicide. Both the outgoing individual who suddenly becomes withdrawn or isolated and the normally reserved individual who suddenly becomes outgoing and thrill-seeking may be at risk for suicide. Such changes are of particular concern when a precipitating painful event has occurred. Poor performance in school such as sudden failure may be an important clue. Making final arrangements like giving away a CD collection, a favorite watch, or other possessions may be ominous and should be recognized as a possible warning sign to teachers. A sudden preoccupation with death, such as reading and talking about death, may

also be a clue. Constructive discussion of this topic as a class project may be helpful, however, for the individual and his/her classmates, since peers are often the first to hear this kind of information.

6. Life-Threatening Behavior: We recall a nine-year-old boy who killed himself. He previously had been seen leaning out of an open window of his apartment, and, at another time, playing with a gun. A 17-year-old teenager died in a single car accident on an isolated road after having had several similar accidents following his mother's death. Self-destructive behavior is not rare. Often alcoholism, drug addiction, mismanagement of physical disease, and auto accidents should be seen for what they might be—suicidal clues. Farberow has called this, "the many faces of suicide" [19]. Here are a number of questions one should consider: Why did the young child, knowing that the gun was loaded and despite his parents' warnings, play with it? Why did the teenager drive so fast on a slippery wet road when he knew that for the last three months his brakes had been bad? Why did a person, knowing the dangers of cocaine use, continue to use it and get hooked? We are not suggesting that these young people intentionally want to die; yet, their behavior made them as "good as dead."

7. Suicide Notes: Like prior suicide attempts and verbal statements, suicidal writings that suggest suicidal ideation are important clues, but, unfortunately, they are often read and ignored by the reader. Such writings are very rare in young children, but more common in adolescents (although most adolescents who kill themselves do not leave a suicide note). Artwork, diaries, music, and other personal documents can be seen as similar expressive clues. One suicide note stated, "I finally completed something I've always wanted to do. I removed the guilt from every person. . . . PS: Happy Father's Day."

Below are a number of genuine suicide notes. They are presented here not merely as a clue but to allow the reader to better understand the mind of young people who actually kill themselves (although we wish to be clear that we would not recommend that such material be presented to students, although it may be useful to adults in a school system to understand better the pain of a suicidal person).

1. Single male, age 13:
   I know what I am doing. Annette, I found out. Ask Carol. I love you all.

2. Single female, age 16:
   Dear Mother & Dad,
   Please forgive me. I have tried to be good to you both. I love you both very much and wanted to get along with you both. I have tried. I have wanted to go out with you & Dad but I was always afraid to ask for I always felt that the answer would be no. And about Bill, I want to dismiss every idea about him. I don't like any more than a compassion, for a while I thought I did not no more, in fact, I am quite tired of him, as you know, I get tired of everyone after a while.

> And mother, I wish you hadn't called me a liar, and said I was just like Hap. As I'm not. It is just that I am afraid of you both at times, but I love you both very much.
>
> So long
Your loving daughter
That will always
love you
Mary
>
> P.S. Please forgive me. I want you to, and don't think for one minute that I haven't appreciated everything you've done.

Although not all young people leave notes or show clues, most do and what is important is that we respond—do something effective!

PREVENTION: WHAT TO DO

The best thing to do when someone's behavior suggests potential suicide risk is to show concern, interest, and support. Yet, most important is to focus on help seeking behavior. Below is a list about what you should do when confronted with suicidal behavior and are concerned about suicide prevention. It is a guide (not a cookbook) for teachers, administrators, and others who are concerned.

1. Believe it. Accept the possibility that your student may be in danger. Take it seriously. Do not deny the possibility because children and teenagers do kill themselves.
2. Check it out. You may want to check with another person (e.g., principal, parent) to see if he/she shares your opinion. Parents may be a good source of information. Often parents (and other students) know what you are only beginning to believe. You may ask the child directly if he/she is thinking of killing him/herself and tell him/her about the clues you have noticed. Suicidal students are often relieved to find someone willing to talk. Don't be afraid that you are putting the thought in his/her mind, even with a child.
3. Be calm. Don't panic. It will only increase the student's perturbation and may jeopardize your own ability to act.
4. Listen. Take the time to listen to your student. Encourage your student to verbalize his/her feelings and thoughts. Accept what he/she says without judgment. Don't make false promises that things will get better immediately. Don't allow yourself to be sworn to secrecy.
5. Show that you care. Make it clear to your student that you understand and are really concerned. Let the child know that you care and want to help in a sound supportive fashion. Make yourself available.
6. Get help. Get professional help. If he or she refuses help, you should initiate it yourself. Contact the parents, the principal, and a professional. Meanwhile, if the risk of suicide is high, don't leave the student alone. Take the student with you along to a source of help or call a crisis center to assist you with what to

do. If the suicidal act is in progress call the ambulance and police immediately. It may be too late to act later if the student has taken some potential life-threatening action.

The main rule is to get help. Whenever a serious suicide risk exists, get immediate help from a trained professional through a suicide prevention center, a school guidance office, a mental health clinic, a family physician, a Samaritan center, or other appropriate services in your area.

If the youngster refuses help and suggests that the parent(s) is the problem, school staff should consult a professional for advice on how to handle the situation. If the youngster requests or demands secrecy, explain and discuss his or her fears but do not swear to secrecy. Our approach, when asked by teachers about this, is to ask them "If it was your son, would you want to know?" Most important, don't delay your actions, get help! Next, we will review the literature on what has helped and what has not.

EVALUATING SCHOOL-BASED PROGRAMS

One of the problems in evaluating school suicide prevention programs is that the programs differ greatly in design and have very different goals. In a survey of school programs, Malley, Kush, and Bogo [20] found that schools reported the following types of programs:

1. written formal policy statements regarding suicide;
2. written procedures for dealing with at-risk students;
3. staff in-service training;
4. mental health professionals at the school;
5. mental health teams at the school;
6. suicide prevention materials for distribution to parents;
7. suicide prevention materials for distribution to students;
8. suicide reference materials for distribution to school counselors;
9. psychological screening programs to identify students at risk for suicide;
10. mental health counseling for students at-risk for suicide;
11. classroom discussions;
12. suicide prevention training for school counselors;
13. suicide prevention training for teachers; and
14. postvention program after student suicides.

Shaffer, Garland, Gould, Fisher, and Trautman have also noted that school-based programs can aim to heighten awareness of the problem, promote case findings, provide staff and pupils with information about mental health resources, and improve the adolescents' coping abilities [21]. As a result, many different criteria have been used to evaluate school-based suicide prevention programs and there appears to be no uniformity forthcoming.

(1) Helping Peers

Kalafat and Gagliano found that, after exposure to their curriculum, students were more likely to seek adult help if a peer was suicidal, and they showed greater concern for a suicidal peer [22]. Kalafat and Elias also found that students exposed to their curriculum developed more positive attitudes toward suicidal peers and were more likely to respond to them in a helpful manner as compared to students not exposed to the curriculum [17].

Abbey, Madsen, and Polland found that their curriculum led to more appropriate helping-responses to suicidal peers in a sample of undergraduates [23].

Ciffone found that students who were given a suicide prevention curriculum developed a more positive attitude toward suicidal people and were more likely to seek help for suicidal peers and themselves as compared to students who did not take the program [24].

Johnson found that students who were given a suicide prevention curriculum were more likely to approach a teacher about a suicidal peer or for themselves after taking the curriculum than before taking it [25]. Nelson found that students who attended a suicide prevention curriculum indicated that they would be more helpful to suicidal peers after the program than they would have been prior to the program [26].

Shaffer, Vieland, Garland, Rojas, Underwood, and Busner [27] and Shaffer, Garland, Vieland, Underwood, and Busner [28] found that students taking a suicide prevention curriculum showed an increase in helpful reactions and responses to a possible suicidal peer than those not taking the course. They did not develop more positive attitudes toward seeking help for general mental health as compared to those not taking the course.

(2) Knowledge About Suicide

Kalafat and Elias found that students exposed to their curriculum acquired greater knowledge about suicidal behavior than those not exposed [17]. Abbey and colleagues gave a program to undergraduate students and found an increase in accurate knowledge about suicide [23]. Nelson reported that his students also had more accurate knowledge after a suicide prevention program and were better able to recognize suicidal clues in others than they did prior to the program [26]. Only 4 percent of the students thought that the program was not helpful for preventing suicide.

Johnson found that teachers given a curriculum on suicide prevention acquired more knowledge than they had before and developed a more positive attitude toward suicidal individuals [25].

Spirito, Overholser, Ashworth, Morgan, and Benedict-Drew [29] and Overholser, Hemstreet, Spirito, and Vyse [30] found that a suicide awareness curriculum increased the students' knowledge about suicide and improved their own coping strategies as compared to students not taking the curriculum. Shaffer and his colleagues found that a suicide prevention curriculum increased the students' knowledge about suicide (although the researchers did not adequately report the scores and the tests of statistical significance) [27, 28]. The students taking the program also showed an increase in knowledge about treatment resources.

(3) Lowering Suicidal Risk

Orbach and Bar-Joseph found that students exposed to their curriculum experienced an improvement in self-reported suicidal tendencies, ego identity, and coping, but not in hopelessness, as compared to students not exposed to the curriculum [31]. No students reported feeling harmed by the program.

Eggert and colleagues ran a program for high school students at high risk for suicide and found no significant differences in their suicidal risk behaviors, depression, and hopelessness as compared to those not in the program [16]. All groups improved whether or not they were in the program.

WHAT DO THE PRINCIPALS THINK?

Miller, Eckert, DuPaul, and White sent secondary school principals a description of one of three possible school-based suicide prevention programs to evaluate [32]. The principals preferred both the curriculum-based program (a two-hour teaching segment for all students during relevant classroom periods) and the staff in-service training program (a two-hour program for staff before the start of the school year) over the school-wide student screening program (in which a suicide potential form was distributed to all students, after which those with high scores would be interviewed by school psychologists). Clearly, for a school-based suicide prevention program to work, it must receive the support of the staff of the school.

AN ECOLOGICAL EVALUATION

Garland, Shaffer, and Whittle surveyed 115 agencies that implemented a school-based curriculum program for students, and they reported the number and proportion of adolescents exposed in each state [33]. Lester compared these numbers with the changes in the suicide rate of 15–19-year-olds in the states [34]. Student participation in the programs was associated with a detrimental effect on state teenage suicide rates. However, Lester found that state government initiatives in addressing youth suicide were associated with a beneficial effect on state teenage suicide rates.

NEGATIVE EFFECTS

Occasional studies have reported negative effects from school-based programs. Spirito and his colleagues [29] and Overholser and his colleagues [30] found that their suicide awareness program increased the hopelessness scores of male students, but not female students, although they also reported positive effects. Shaffer and his colleagues found that students participating in their suicide prevention program were more likely to see suicide as a solution to problems after the course, especially male students and black students [27, 28]. They also found that 7 percent of the students found the program "upsetting." In particular, Shaffer and his colleagues found that students who had previously attempted suicide were more negative about the program for their friends (not themselves) than students who had never attempted suicide (although the majority of both groups were positive about the program), and they were more likely to report knowing someone who was upset by the program. The attempters were also more likely to state that the program had made it harder for them to deal with friends' problems. It is likely, based on the data in the study, that these attempters did not like the fact that their friends learned that they were troubled and may be suffering from psychopathology. Furthermore, although over all the students there was an increase in accurate knowledge about suicide and a more positive attitude toward seeking help, these effects were not found for the small subgroup (7 percent of the sample) that had previously attempted suicide. Of course, an obvious interpretation of these results is that attempters may not only not appreciate their friends learning about their psychopathology and problems in life, but do not want to accept the seriousness of their pain. It is obvious to us that this is all the more reason to provide education to all in the schools, as these youngsters will likely continue to be at risk.

THE OPINIONS OF EXPERTS

Eddy, Wolpert, and Rosenberg asked 15 experts on youth suicide to rank various preventive measures for their usefulness [35]. Although there was a wide variation in the experts' ranking, school-based screening ranked third-equal, along with improved treatment, but behind restricting access to firearms and identifying high-risk youth.

A CONCLUDING REMARK

Suicide and suicidal behavior in youth is not uncommon and, although most of us will never experience these events in our own schools, it is important that all of us have a basic understanding of suicide risk and what to do in critical situations. Schools can support efforts in helping a suicidal person and in making sure that professional help is obtained, which may very likely save a life. Teachers must recognize their role as potential supporters and can readily learn appropriate ways of dealing with suicidal young people. Teachers need to know basics in prevention. All of us have a role in this education. The belief that suicide prevention works only temporarily is a myth. Research basically supports a school-based strategy. With appropriate social support, whether it is about suicide prevention or AIDS education and so on, students can be assisted to live long, fulfilling lives.

REFERENCES

1. P. Friedman (ed.), *On Suicide,* International University Press, New York, 1967. (Original work published in 1910.)
2. J. Glidewell and C. Swallow, *The Prevalence of Maladjustment in Elementary Schools,* University of Chicago Press, Chicago, 1969.
3. J. Durlak, *School-Based Prevention Programs for Children and Adolescents,* Sage, Thousand Oaks, California, 1995.
4. R. Diekstra, The Epidemiology of Suicide and Parasuicide, *Archives of Suicide Research, 2,* pp. 1-29, 1996.
5. C. Pfeffer, *The Suicidal Child,* Guilford, New York, 1986.
6. A. Berman and D. Jobes, *Adolescent Suicide: Assessment and Intervention,* American Psychological Press, Washington, D.C., 1991.
7. D. Lester, *The Cruelest Death: The Enigma of Adolescent Suicide,* Charles Press, Philadelphia, 1993.
8. A. Leenaars and S. Wenckstern (eds.), *Suicide Prevention in Schools,* Hemisphere, Washington, D.C., 1990.
9. E. Shneidman, *Definition of Suicide,* Wiley, New York, 1985.
10. A. Leenaars and S. Wenckstern, Suicide Prevention in Schools: The Art, Issues and Pitfalls, *Crisis, 20,* pp. 132-142, 1999.
11. A. Kazdin, Psychotherapy for Children and Adolescents, *Annual Review of Psychology, 41,* pp. 21-54, 1990.
12. A. Leenaars, Suicide Postvention in a School System, *Canada's Mental Health, 33,* pp. 29-30, 1985.
13. G. Martin, Media Influence to Suicide: The Search for Solutions, *Archives of Suicide Research, 4,* pp. 51-66, 1998.
14. G. Caplan, *Principles of Preventive Psychiatry,* Basic Books, New York, 1964.
15. E. Shneidman, Suicide, *Encyclopedia Britannica,* Vol. 21, William Benton, Chicago, pp. 383-385, 1973.
16. L. L. Eggert, E. A. Thompson, J. R. Herting, and L. J. Nicholas, Reducing Suicide Potential among High-Risk Youth, *Suicide & Life-Threatening Behavior, 25,* pp. 276-296, 1995.
17. J. Kalafat and M. Elias, An Evaluation of a School-Based Suicide Awareness Intervention, *Suicide & Life-Threatening Behavior, 24,* pp. 224-233, 1994.
18. C. King, Suicidal Behavior in Adolescence, in *Review of Suicidology,* R. Maris, M. Silverman, and S. Canetto (eds.), Guilford, New York, pp. 61-95, 1997.
19. N. Farberow, *The Many Faces of Suicide,* McGraw-Hill, New York, 1980.

20. P. B. Malley, F. Kush, and R. J. Bogo, School-Based Adolescent Suicide Prevention and Intervention Programs, *School Counselor, 42,* pp. 130-136, 1994.
21. D. Shaffer, A. Garland, M. Gould, P. Fisher, and P. Trautman, Preventing Teenage Suicide, *Journal of the American Academy of Child & Adolescent Psychiatry, 27,* pp. 675-687, 1988.
22. J. Kalafat and C. Gagliano, The Use of Simulations to Assess the Impact of an Adolescent Suicide Response Curriculum, *Suicide & Life-Threatening Behavior, 26,* pp. 359-364, 1996.
23. K. J. Abbey, C. H. Madsen, and R. Polland, Short-Term Suicide Awareness Curriculum, *Suicide & Life-Threatening Behavior, 19,* pp. 216-227, 1989.
24. J. Ciffone, Suicide Prevention, *Social Work, 38,* pp. 197-203, 1993.
25. W. Johnson, Classroom Discussion of Suicide, *Contemporary Education, 56,* pp. 114-117, 1985.
26. F. L. Nelson, Evaluation of a Youth Suicide Prevention School Program, *Adolescence, 88,* pp. 813-825, 1987.
27. D. Shaffer, V. Vieland, A. Garland, M. Rojas, M. Underwood, and C. Busner, Adolescent Suicide Attempters, *Journal of the American Medical Association, 264,* pp. 3151-3155, 1990.
28. D. Shaffer, A. Garland, V. Vieland, M. Underwood, and C. Busner, The Impact of Curriculum-Based Suicide Prevention Program for Teenagers, *Journal of the American Academy of Child & Adolescent Psychiatry, 30,* pp. 588-596, 1991.
29. A. Spirito, J. Overholser, S. Ashworth, J. Morgan, and T. Benedict-Drew, Evaluation of a Suicide Awareness Curriculum for High School Students, *Journal of the American Academy of Child & Adolescent Psychiatry, 27,* pp. 705-711, 1988.
30. J. C. Overholser, A. H. Hemstreet, A. Spirito, and S. Vyse, Suicide Awareness Programs in the Schools, *Journal of the American Academy of Child & Adolescent Psychiatry, 28,* pp. 925-930, 1989.
31. I. Orbach and H. Bar-Joseph, The Impact of a Suicide Prevention Program for Adolescents on Suicidal Tendencies, Hopelessness, Ego Identity, and Coping, *Suicide & Life-Threatening Behavior, 23,* pp. 120-129, 1993.
32. D. N. Miller, T. L. Eckert, G. J. DuPaul, and G. P. White, Adolescent Suicide Prevention, *Suicide & Life-Threatening Behavior, 29,* pp. 72-85, 1999.
33. A. Garland, D. Shaffer, and B. Whittle, A National Survey of School-Based, Adolescent Suicide Prevention Programs, *Journal of the American Academy of Child & Adolescent Psychiatry, 28,* pp. 931-934, 1989.
34. D. Lester, State Initiatives in Addressing Youth Suicide, *Social Psychiatry & Psychiatric Epidemiology, 27,* pp. 75-77, 1992.
35. D. M. Eddy, R. L. Wolpert, and M. L. Rosenberg, Estimating the Effectiveness of Interventions to Prevent Youth Suicide, *Medical Care, 25*:12(Suppl), pp. S57-S65, 1987.

CHAPTER 10

Social Support in Suicide Postvention

Susanne Wenckstern and Antoon A. Leenaars

Postvention refers to those things done after a trauma such as a suicide has occurred [1]. Postvention deals with the traumatic after-effects in the survivors. Schools/communities are an especially critical force in such endeavors with our youth [Centers for Disease Control (CDC), since renamed Centers for Disease Control and Prevention, 2].

Leenaars provided the first documented conceptual model in the literature, in the last century, for postvention in schools and their communities, namely one of an acute stress and posttraumatic stress perspective [3, see also 4, 5]. Suicide is a trauma for the survivors [6], a view supported by research [7-9]. Freud, in 1917, already noted that loss of a significant other (related primarily to attachment) results in a traumatic response, with special symptoms of depression [10]. Indeed, from his clinical records, Freud had noted that the greater the degree of trauma, the greater the distress. He described the response as a developmental sequence to trauma [11]. This is especially true for suicide since there is almost no other death in our society for which there is a higher social (and often personal dynamic) stigma for the survivors. Thus, it is heuristic to view the event from the acute stress and post-traumatic stress framework.

While there are victims of many and diverse traumatic events [12], including of suicide [3], there are common psychological responses to trauma. Recognition of the commonalities was furthered, in 1980, by the American Psychiatric Association's (APA's) DSM-III [13]; post-traumatic stress disorder (PTSD) was introduced as a new classification. The DSM-III spelled out characteristic symptoms that may follow "a psychologically traumatic event that is generally outside the range of usual human experience." PTSD was first associated in the 1900s with the trauma of military combat, particularly the victims of the Vietnam War [14]. However, as Janoff-Bulman (1985) pointed out, PTSD can be equally associated with a large variety of traumatic events (e.g., serious crimes, homicide, accidents, disasters) [12]. Suicide is clearly outside the usual human experience and, indeed, evokes "significant symptoms of distress in most people" [15, 16].

Traumatic stress response refers to those natural behaviors and emotions that occur during a catastrophe. Figley defined a *post*-traumatic stress response "as a set of conscious and unconscious behaviors and emotions associated with dealing with the memories of the stressors of the catastrophe and immediately afterwards" [17]. These are common aftershocks and by no means do all or even most survivors exhibit the necessary characteristics of such a reaction to be labeled a disorder, i.e., PTSD [17]. We intend here, rather, to use PTSD as a heuristic label since it approximates best the reaction in survivors of suicide and trauma in our schools/communities. In addition to the existence of a recognized stressor, symptoms of the aftershocks may include the following: reexperiencing of the trauma (e.g., recurrent recollection, recurrent dreams, associations that the event is recurring); numbing of responsiveness to a reduced involvement with the external world (e.g., diminished interest, detachment, constricted affect); and various other symptoms: depression, grief, hyperalertness, sleep disturbance, survivor guilt, problems in memory/concentration, avoidance of events that evoke recall, intensification of symptoms by events that symbolize events, to name a few. An important observation made by Janoff-Bulman in 1985 [12] about PTSD is the following: that "much of the psychological trauma produced by victimizing events derives from the shattering of very basic assumptions that victims have held about the operation of the world." We all have constructs, a theory of the world, for example: "Johnny, the ten year old, doesn't kill himself." With Johnny's suicide, our view of the world may be shattered, resulting in possible PTSD. We have to cope with "Johnny killed himself."

PTSD was initially intended for adults [13]. Eth and Pynoos, however, presented convincing evidence for application of PTSD to children and adolescents [18]. Children of trauma exhibit such symptoms as "deleterious effects on cognition (including memory, school performance, and learning), affect, interpersonal relations, impulse control, aggressive behavior, vegetative function, and the formulation of symptoms" [18, p. 41]. In some classical studies, Terr [19], as well as Lifton and Olson [20], observed that there is a post-traumatic reaction in abducted children and in children surviving a disaster (e.g., Hiroshima). There are amazing commonalities in how children respond to various unusual trauma [6]. Bowlby suggested that the most important is anxious attachment behavior [21]. Children may not appear to exhibit a reaction (e.g., there are few recognizable overt verbalizations), but there may well be a negative one, often fostered by an adult who also wants to deny the trauma. Responders seem to minimize the psychological nature of acute stress and post-traumatic stress in young people. Years ago, Anna Freud noted that children frequently rely on various forms of denial to respond to trauma, evident in fantasy, action, and affect, all to ease (numb) the pain [22]. Alcohol and drug use are obvious examples in teens. In response to such observations, in 1987 the APA clarified its definition to include children and teens [23].

Adjusting to a trauma is remarkably difficult. Freud distinguished between positive and negative reactions to trauma [24]. He saw remembering, repeating, and reexperiencing as positive, whereas he saw forgetting, avoidance, phobia, and inhibition as negative. These latter negative approaches are, however, common in many victims after a suicide (and other traumas), even in adults who are to guide our youngsters, such as principals, psychologists, etc. A common response is to deny it: "Don't talk about it; after all, talking about suicide causes suicide." We firmly believe, as has been so well documented with Vietnam victims, that this approach only exacerbates the trauma. However, as Wilson and colleagues have pointed out, it is important for us to see that the victims of a suicide (even the principal, psychologist, etc.) may be caught in a no-win cycle of events [9]. They note the following:

> To talk about the powerful and overwhelming trauma means risking further stigmatization; the failure to discuss the traumatic episode increases the need for defensive avoidance and thus increases the probability of depression alternating with cycles of intensive imagery and other symptoms of PTSD [9, p. 169].

Survivors need social support after a trauma. Positive adjustive strategies need to be fostered by the social system, such as schools.

One of our main contentions is that postvention in schools/communities should be designed to address not only suicide but other traumas as well [see 25 for details]. This belief re-arose in 1999 for the junior author when the murders-suicides occurred in Littleton's Columbine High School. Regrettably, few saw that event as a suicide event. The same was true of the kindergarten murders-suicide in Dunblane, Scotland. These events are often treated as an event of lethal violence, which they are, but they are more—they are also a suicidal event. The junior author recalled discussing the issue years ago with a bureaucrat from the government after Canada's best-known suicide, Lepine, murdered 14 females and then killed himself at the Polytechnical School in Montreal, in 1989. The bureaucrat's response, when the issue was raised, was, "Oh, now you want to claim this too," and then he added, "like the women have." Of course, one could say that this is only the reaction of one naïve bureaucrat; yet, regrettably his view is one shared by many, including by some administrators in schools. Lepine was a suicide and so were Columbine High School's students, Harris and Kliebold. Harris, for example, had a history of isolation, had been treated for depression and had planned his death. The tenet is: until we recognize that these events are among other things, suicides, we will not respond as effectively as possible in our postventions.

Harris, Lepine, and individuals like them feel rejected and angry. Since the discussion on youth suicide in 1910 in Freud's home in Vienna, aggression has been seen as a core element in understanding suicide [26]. Freud, in fact, saw murder and suicide as interwoven [10]. In the earliest empirical studies of suicide, Shneidman and Farberow discovered both anger directed toward self and others in suicide notes [27]. Suicide may be murder in the 180th degree and in a few, first a murder [16, 28]

The murder-suicide hypothesis of suicide is often neglected, especially in the media. This taboo is even more lamentable than simply addressing, say Columbine, because as Cantor, Sheehan, Alpers, and Mullen have recently shown, these murder-suicide events may impact on subsequent murder-suicide, even 10 years later [29]. Eight days after Columbine, for example, a 15-year-old youth gunned down students, killing one, in M. R. Myers High School in Taber, Canada. The boy was obsessed with Columbine and, like Harris, was isolated, bullied, depressed, and under psychiatric care. Cantor and colleagues hypothesized that the sensational reporting by the media is a core factor in such imitations. The factors, however, are diverse and relate to our lack of response to the complexity of aggressive acts of both murder and self-murder.

We must be prepared to respond to trauma in our schools. At the very least, this includes clearer understanding of what our very definition of trauma is. Littleton was a complex trauma and among other things, it was a suicidal event. If we are to address the aftershocks of such traumas, we must respond to this fact, known almost 100 years ago [26]. Postvention hopefully will be more insightful into the complexity of suicide and trauma in the future, otherwise, as Cantor and colleagues showed, we will have more murder-suicides in our schools and communities [29].

STRATEGIES FOR POSTVENTION

Given the complexity of traumatic reactions, the response to suicide and trauma in schools/communities must be equally complex. Simple social supports must be avoided, and, thus, we can only offer here a few highlights, lest we commit a similar error. More comprehensive discussion of the strategies for postvention is presented elsewhere [3, 5, 6, 25, 30, 31]. At the very least, the essential strategies appear to be the following:

1. Consultation

Discussion, coordination, and planning are undertaken at every phase, beginning with school administration and then followed by school staff and other involved individuals, such as students and parents, under the direction of the postvention coordinator, that is, a mental health expert who takes charge and provides structure. Community personnel may need to be included during every sequence of the process to provide needed social supports, depending on the evaluation of the mild-moderate-severe level of the traumatic event [32]. Concurrent peer consultation and review among professional staff that are involved in the postvention program (postvention team) are undertaken to review the plans that were implemented and to plan and coordinate further action. For example, a flexible contingency plan must be preplanned to allow for alternative actions, if needed. Territorial problems between school and community (and their own internal politics) need to be addressed since often these are the very elements that raise the traumatic levels of the event.

2. Crisis Intervention

Emergency or crisis response is provided, using basic problem solving strategies. We believe that students and staff of the local school(s) are likely to need support in response to a suicide trauma. It is crucial not to underestimate the closeness of relationships or the intensity of reactions of individuals who might be experiencing post-traumatic reactions [1, 4, 33-38].

3. Community Linkage

As we believe it is imperative that survivors of suicide and other traumas be provided with the appropriate support, we assist these individuals to obtain such services. Educational systems need to develop a linkage system or network to aid in making referrals to the appropriate community services and to exchange information and coordinate services with appropriate community services as needed. Such a network is central to responding to a trauma and should be predefined. No individual/system can address all the needs, a problem that is especially evident in contracted service. It is highly recommended that postventionists become familiar with and update local community resources on an ongoing basis before a traumatic event such as suicide occurs, for example, knowing which agency or service to contact and preferably the name of the contact person (e.g., police, ambulance, hospital emergency). For culturally different students, having a directory on hand listing local cultural centers and names of translators, with preestablished communications, may be not only very helpful but a necessity.

4. Assessment and Counseling

Evaluation and therapy are provided as needed or requested by the postventionists or the school administrator, for example, the principal or his or her designate. Assessment, as we already noted, is complex but can be approximated [39, 40]. Psychotherapy is equally complicated and, contrary to current efforts, often must be long term—and in some cases, will call for medication and even hospitalization. Adolescents at risk, for example, are often suffering long-term pain that has undermined their ego. We strongly believe since our first postvention effort that once students are identified, that treatment should be individual, not in groups. Groups may serve the initial task of response to a shared trauma, but the student in need should be referred to a therapist for scheduled appointments as soon as possible. One needs to defuse the aftershock, not add to the hysteria [41, 42]. An outline for psychotherapy has been presented elsewhere [37, 38].

5. Education

Information about suicide and its prevention (e.g., clues, myths, causes, what to do, where to go for help, etc.) is provided through discussion, seminars, workshops, and small assemblies/classes (20–30 people) at the school and within the community [4]. This aspect of the program, based on the current literature, is prevention and that topic is so vast that we can only remark on it here. As a final note, educational programs should be undertaken after the aftershocks are normalized, not as part of the early crisis intervention.

6. Liaison with the media

Information about suicide in the form of publicity, especially that which tends to sensationalize or glamorize the suicide, should be avoided. It is not and should not be the school's responsibility to provide information about the actuarial details of the suicide, as in any trauma, to the media. This falls within the jurisdiction of the police department, coroner's office, or other authorities. However, our experience has shown us that 1) a media spokesperson for the school must be appointed at the outset of the crisis, and 2) this role should be filled by the postvention coordinator and not by a school administrator (e.g., the principal). Not only does this ensure the accuracy and consistency of information being given out, but also most important, it ensures that this information is being provided by someone who understands the postvention procedures and positive impact of the program. It is the procedures, e.g., focusing on positive social support, and their impact that should be emphasized to the media.

7. Follow-Up

Periodic follow-ups are undertaken with the school administrators, school staff, and mental health professionals. A formal final consultation and evaluation is provided several months after the suicide to facilitate a formal closure to the program. Our experience has shown that such consultations and reviews should be supportive in character (e.g., "What did we do?"; "What helped/didn't help?"; "What other things might we have considered?") Assaultive and overly critical reviews (e.g., "Did you do _____?", "Why did/didn't you do _____?", etc.) are of little help. A supportive approach from the first contact to follow-up is most helpful, albeit we should not eschew constructive feedback. However, every attempt is made to let all concerned know that the postventionists are available on request for follow-up if the need arises. Obviously, postvention is not the only aspect of these strategies. Such a view is too limited, nor is it scientifically sound to evaluate the impact of suicide postvention by, for example, a paper and pencil follow-up of one group, such as students, of such endeavors.

PRINCIPLES OF POSTVENTION

Shneidman has provided us with some principles of postvention that are ubiquitous (common) in responding to the post suicide event [1]. Shneidman's work was largely based on his extensive work with survivors in a psycho-therapeutic context. Those principles have been modified for application within schools and their community settings, and are here presented in an abbreviated form (refer to Leenaars and Wenckstern [5] for a complete discussion).

1. In working with survivor victims of suicide, it is best to begin as soon as possible after the tragedy, within the first 24 hours if that can be managed.

Consultation and networking between all concerned personnel at a school (e.g., administrators, teachers, and mental health professionals acting under the direction of a postvention coordinator) are critical at this time. Response must be as prompt as possible; waiting even 24 hours can exacerbate the trauma. It is important to compile and share accurate, reliable information about the event, as it becomes known, particularly to combat hysteria. Hysteria often mounts when misinformation, frequently of a sensational nature, proliferates. In these early moments of postvention, it is imperative to strive to establish structure and clear lines of communication as quickly and as effectively as possible.

2. Resistance may be met from the survivors; some—but not all—are either willing or eager to have the opportunity to talk to professionally-oriented persons.

To survive a traumatic event may be painful, and for some people, very painful. Therefore, resistance is understandable and, in fact, is to be expected. Yet, individuals, not only the victim but even the responder, may wish to deny the reality of the traumatic event or of its implications. Experience has shown that this resistance may come not only from child or teen survivors but also from a source that is essential in the cooperative effort of postvention: administration and colleagues. For example, people who have experienced a traumatic event may feel angry, injured, or rejected in any or all of the following circumstances: when they have had to wait for help for an excessive period (24 hours; even 1 hour!); when they are offered inadequate rapport, interest, and so on; when they are dealt with too directly; when they are disappointed by a postventionist who forgets important details or who confronts them about an issue too early; when they are offered only an inadequate intervention (e.g., a 1-hour group meeting) or are left feeling "cut off" by premature termination of assistance; when they are referred to others without adequate explanation of the process or of the reasons for the referral; when they are approached with procedures that are not age appropriate; or when they are contacted by unfamiliar persons other than those involved in the postvention process.

Similarly, the postventionist must be aware of possible denial in himself or herself. It may be unhelpful or even dangerous, for example, when postventionists: underestimate the seriousness of the trauma; are overwhelmed by their own feelings of guilt, incompetence, anxiety, fear, and anger; are unwilling to discuss posttrauma aftershocks or view cries for help solely as manipulative efforts; allow themselves to be lulled into a false sense of security by statements from survivors that everything is fine (e.g., when a principal denies the impact of the event and refuses to allow a postvention response in the school setting); are unable to identify or access appropriate resources required by a particular event (e.g., a homicide/suicide in the school); or fail to persuade survivors to obtain additional assistance that they need.

3. Negative emotions about the decedent (the deceased person) or about any trauma—irritation, anger, fear, shame, guilt, and so on—need to be explored, but not at the very beginning. Timing is critical.

Negative emotions are to be expected after an unusual, traumatic event. Despite commonalities, differences occur in young people's responses to a trauma due to developmental age [18, 43]. Simply stated, a child of five reacts differently than the 12 year old. Children at these ages express negative emotion differently. By the time a person is an adolescent, post-traumatic reactions increasingly resemble those seen in adults.

Moreover, individual children will respond differently to similar events. The greatest risk of complications appears to occur in children who identify most closely with the dead person [44]. Thus, it is important "to specify how the nature and complexity of the stressor event impacts on the unique personality of the survivor" [9, pp. 167-168). Child and teen survivors are not all alike; they bring with them their own special ways of adjusting to trauma. Some teens and children may become at risk for suicide [28].

The critical question in all postvention is whether or not the environment is socially supportive [17]. Not surprisingly, "more supportive environments tend to be associated with better adjustment to stress" [45, p. 61]. Even in our elementary schools, some adults foster denial and unwittingly promote negative adjustment by failing to explore children's reactions to traumatic events or by addressing them at the wrong time or in the wrong way(s). Constructive strategies, as those outlined, need to implemented, with adequate training for all in the same, beginning with the school administration, followed by school staff and other involved adults.

As survivors of a traumatic event such as a suicide, youth at risk for suicide themselves may feel boxed in, rejected, deprived, forlorn, and distressed. In particular, feelings of hopelessness and helplessness may lead to a sense of painful impotence. These young people desperately want a way out [46, 47]. Suicide may appear to be *the* solution to a problem. Moreover, a child is, of course, insufficiently developed to cope with the trauma and its associated pain. The child's ego—the part of the mind that reacts to reality and has a sense of individuality—is not sufficiently developed. Such children at risk lack constructive tendencies; their ego is weakened and this correlates positively with suicide risk.

The role of the postventionist is to anticipate suicide or other unhealthy behaviors in the aftermath of a traumatic event, to identify the presence of these tendencies when they actually do occur, to work to mitigate their likelihood or gravity, and to offer constructive alternatives as appropriate. In circumstances when life seems to have rejected a child and caused extreme hurt, the postventionist offers acceptance, care, and love.

4. Unwarranted optimism or banal platitudes should be avoided in postvention.

We often hear adults say the following: "Don't talk about the trauma, it will go away"; Don't worry, we will save you"; "All people respond in the same way, we will tell you how they will react"; "Postvention is the same as prevention"; or "Postvention is only grief counseling." All of these and other similar statements are banal platitudes. Denial will not make the trauma go away. One hour of group counseling with 30 students is not postvention. Unrealistic optimism makes the aftershocks worse. Postvention is complex work requiring sensitivity, imagination, and dedication [3, 6, 25].

5. Trauma work is multifaceted and takes a while—anywhere from several months to the end of a person's life.

The multifaceted character of postvention arises from the potential complexity of traumatic events on the one hand, as well as the multidimensional character and individuality of human responses to those events on the other hand. Simply stated, there is no room for simple solutions. This multifaceted characteristic of postvention is often not understood, even by professionals and researchers. This reality can be illustrated by the recent research of Hazell and Lewin [48]. These authors sought to evaluate postvention by examining suicide cases in two schools, albeit with limitations. Hazell and Lewin equated postvention with group counseling. Yet, postvention does not simply equal group counseling. Group counseling can be one strategy of postvention, although we firmly believe that individual work is a more appropriate primary mode of treatment. Hazell and Lewin evaluated only increase in risk; however, contagion is only one possible aftershock. They developed a risk index for suicide, to measure the aftershocks, which itself is questionable according to a recent review by the National Institute of Mental Health [49, 50]. Group counseling in the situations examined by Hazell and Lewin also presents problems because it consisted of seeing 20 to 30 children in a group for 90 minutes. Hazell and Lewin concluded that postvention does not work and schools should not implement such programs.

Regrettably, some people have now argued that postvention is useless. Postvention must be based on sound research. The same issue has arisen in the field of education in the schools about suicide and death. From a methodologically unsound study, Shaffer, Garland, Vieland, Underwood, and Busner concluded that there should be *no* primary prevention in schools [51]. However, developing research [e.g., 52] has shown the value of prevention. We believe the same is true about postvention and we encourage sound research in the field to be able to respond better to trauma in schools and their communities, especially since postvention work is multifaceted.

6. A comprehensive program of health care on the part of a benign and enlightened community should include prevention, intervention, and postvention.

As a response to its awareness of the complexity of postvention, the CDC in the United States developed a set of comprehensive guidelines for postvention with special attention to suicide "contagion" or clustering [2]. These guidelines incorporate aspects of prevention, intervention, and postvention as equally essential. Among these guidelines, the following points can be adapted to our present discussion.

A community and its schools should develop plans for responding to traumatic events before they occur. These plans should include the following:

- All concerned individuals should be involved in the response, along with leadership from a mental health coordinator, the postventionist.
- The response should be initiated promptly after a traumatic event.
- The response should begin with coordination.
- Constructive relationships should be developed with the media, and efforts should be made to avoid sensationalism in any form.
- Children, teens, and others who are at risk for suicide or other complicated responses to the traumatic event should be identified and referred for individual therapy.
- Potentially harmful aspects of the environment should be identified and changed.
- Long-term issues should be addressed.

These suggestions are inherent in any sound program of postvention.

The CDC recognized that no universal rules apply for all postvention situations. Both the principles noted here and the suggestions provided by the CDC are guidelines. They are meant to provide schools and communities with "a conceptual framework for developing their own . . . [postvention] plans, adapted to the particular needs, resources, and cultural characteristics of their communities" [2, p. 2].

CASE ILLUSTRATION

As an illustration of the complexity, we hereby provide a case illustration. The senior author was involved in a double suicide postvention response at a high school, where both suicides were students who were well known to the student body, school staff, and surrounding community in general. Several community agencies were contacted after the event became known, to assist in providing needed community support to the large number of individuals/groups in need, as well as to provide necessary assistance/support to the postvention team. The critical importance of social support was immediately apparent to all involved persons. In this case, for example, these two students committed suicide together toward the end of the week; hence (as tends to be the norm in our culture), funeral visitation times were on the weekend, at different funeral homes; yet, at similar, common visitation times. The two funeral homes involved collaborated and tried to sensitively coordinate funeral services in an attempt to meet the needs of a variety of people, including the two families, relatives, and sets of friends. Despite these efforts, in a very practical way, this proved very difficult for a number of student peers and friends in particular, who needed to visit at both funeral homes and attend both funerals. Numerous people came out on that difficult weekend to provide whatever support they could, e.g., school administrators, teachers, other school staff, parents, clergy, and so on. Members of the postvention team took shifts at the funeral homes during that long weekend to provide ongoing support and assistance to the survivors. A similar plan of coverage was undertaken for the funeral services. During the funeral service, one of the officiating clergymen addressed the suicide nature of the deaths openly and directly, as well as constructively. This approach helped to significantly promote even greater social support and the beginning of healing for many of the survivors. In the following weeks at the high school, aside from providing counseling and follow-up with a number of students and their families, plans were carefully considered with regard to having available support present before, during, and after that high school's graduation ceremony, which occurred shortly after the suicides. This experience became for some team members a realization, and for other team members a potent reminder, of the complexity of postvention, and the complex interwoveness of the school with its community.

CONCLUDING REMARKS

Suicide and other traumas do occur in our children and youth and in our schools/communities. We need to provide survivors of suicide and other traumas with positive, appropriate supports. The belief that postvention only makes things worse is a myth. Research supports the importance of positive social supports in postvention. Doing postvention in schools is doing postvention within the community—with all of its people. We all need to have a basic understanding of basic postvention strategies and principles, and specifically what teachers, administrators, psychologists, and others can do to help support the survivors.

REFERENCES

1. E. Shneidman, Postvention: The Care for the Bereaved, in *Suicide Thoughts and Reflections,* E. Shneidman (ed.), Human Sciences Press, New York, 1981.
2. Centers for Disease Control (CDC), *Recommendations for a Community Plan for the Prevention and Containment of Suicide Clusters,* MMWR, 37 (Suppl. no. S-6), Author, Washington, D.C., 1988.
3. A. Leenaars, Suicide Postvention in a School System, *Canada's Mental Health, 33*:4, 1985.
4. A. Leenaars and S. Wenckstern (eds.), *Suicide Prevention in Schools,* Hemisphere, Washington, D.C., 1990.
5. A. Leenaars and S. Wenckstern, Principles of Postvention: Application to Suicide and Trauma in Schools, *Death Studies, 22,* pp. 357-391, 1998.
6. A. Leenaars and S. Wenckstern, Post-Traumatic Stress Disorder: A Conceptual Model for Postvention, in *Suicide Prevention in Schools,* A. Leenaars and S. Wenckstern (eds.), Hemisphere, Washington, D.C., pp. 173-180, 1990.
7. G. Gleser, B. Green, and C. Wignet, *Buffalo Creek Revisited: Prolonged Psychosocial Effects of Disaster,* Simon & Schuster, New York, 1981.
8. M. Horowitz, Psychological Response to Serious Life Events, in *Human Stress and Cognition,* V. Hamilton and D. Warburton (eds.), Wiley, New York, 1979.
9. J. Wilson, W. Smith, and S. Johnson, A Comparative Analysis of PTSD among Various Survivor Groups, in *Trauma and Its Wake,* C. Figley (ed.), Brunner/Mazel, New York, pp. 142-173, 1985.
10. S. Freud, Introductory Lectures in Psychoanalysis, in *The Standard Edition of the Complete Psychological Works of Sigmund Freud, Vol. XVI,* J. Strachey (trans. and ed.), Hogarth, London, 1974. (Original published in 1917.)
11. S. Freud, Inhibitions, Symptoms and Anxiety, in *The Standard Edition of the Complete Psychological Works of Sigmund Freud, Vol. XX,* J. Strachey (ed. and trans.), Hogarth, London, 1974. (Original published in 1926.)
12. R. Janoff-Bulman, The Aftermath of Victimization: Rebuilding Shattered Assumptions, in *Trauma and Its Wake,* C. Figley (ed.), Brunner/Mazel, New York, pp. 15-35, 1985.
13. American Psychiatric Association, *Diagnostic and Statistical Manual of Mental Disorders* (3rd Edition), Author, Washington, D.C., 1980.
14. C. Figley (ed.), *Stress Disorders among Vietnam Veterans,* Brunner/Mazel, New York, 1978.
15. A. Leenaars, *Suicide Notes,* Human Sciences Press, New York, 1988.
16. E. Shneidman, *Definition of Suicide,* Wiley, New York, 1985.
17. C. Figley, Introduction, in *Trauma and Its Wake,* Brunner/Mazel, New York, pp. xvii-xxvi, 1985.
18. G. Eth and R. Pynoos, *Post-Traumatic Stress Disorder in Children,* American Psychiatric Press, Inc., Washington, D.C., 1985.
19. L. Terr, Children of Chonchilla: Study of Psychic Trauma, *Psychoanalytic Study of the Child, 34,* pp. 547-623, 1979.

20. R. Lifton and E. Olson, The Human Meaning of Total Disaster: The Buffalo Creek Experience, *Psychiatry, 133,* pp. 306-312, 1976.
21. J. Bowlby, The Making and Breaking of Affectionate Bonds, *British Journal of Psychiatry, 130*, pp. 201-208, 421-431, 1977.
22. A. Freud, *Ego and Mechanism of Defense,* International Universities Press, New York, 1966.
23. American Psychiatric Association, *Diagnostic and Statistical Manual of Mental Disorders* (3rd Edition, Revised), Author, Washington, D.C., 1987.
24. S. Freud, Moses and Monotheism, in *The Standard Edition of the Complete Psychological Works of Sigmund Freud, Vol. XXIII,* J. Strachey (ed. and trans), Hogarth, London, 1974. (Original published in 1939.)
25. S. Wenckstern and A. Leenaars, Trauma and Suicide in Schools, *Death Studies, 17,* pp. 253-266, 1993.
26. P. Friedman (ed.), *On Suicide,* International Universities Press, New York, 1967. (Original published in 1910.)
27. E. Shneidman and N. Farberow (eds.), *Clues to Suicide,* McGraw-Hill, New York, 1957.
28. A. Leenaars, Suicide: A Multidimensional Malaise, *Suicide and Life-Threatening Behavior, 26,* pp. 221-236, 1996.
29. C. Cantor, P. Sheehan, P. Alpers, and P. Mullen, Media and Mass Homicide, *Archives of Suicide Research, 5,* pp. 283-290, 1999.
30. A. Leenaars and S. Wenckstern, Postvention with Elementary School Children, in *Handbook of Childhood Death and Bereavement,* C. Corr and D. Corr (eds.), Springer, New York, pp. 265-283, 1996.
31. S. Wenckstern and A. Leenaars, Suicide Postvention in a Secondary School, in *Suicide Prevention in Schools,* A. Leenaars and S. Wenckstern (eds.), Hemisphere, Washington, D.C., pp. 181-195, 1990.
32. L. Goodstein, *Consulting with Human Services Systems,* Addison-Wesley, Menlo Park, California, 1978.
33. G. Caplan, *Principles of Preventive Psychiatry,* Basic Books, New York, 1964.
34. N. Farberow, Crisis, Disaster, and Suicide: Theory and Therapy, in *Essays in Self-Destruction,* E. Shneidman (ed.), Science House, Inc., New York, pp. 373-398, 1967.
35. L. Hoff, *People in Crisis* (2nd edition), Addison-Wesley, Menlo Park, California, 1984.
36. L. Hoff, Crisis Intervention in Schools, in *Suicide Prevention in Schools,* A Leenaars and S. Wenckstern (eds.), Hemisphere, Washington, D.C., pp. 123-134, 1990.
37. A. Leenaars, Crisis Intervention with Highly Lethal Suicidal People, *Death Studies, 18,* pp. 341-360, 1994.
38. A. Leenaars, J. Maltsberger, and R. Neimeyer (eds.), *Treatment of Suicidal People,* Taylor & Francis, Washington, D.C., 1994.
39. A. Leenaars, Clinical Evaluation of Suicide Risk, *Japanese Journal of Psychiatry and Neurology, 49*(Suppl 1), pp. 561-568, 1995.
40. R. Maris, A. Berman, J. Maltsberger, and R. Yufit (eds.), *Assessment and Prediction of Suicide,* Guilford, New York, 1992.
41. J. Callahan, Negative Effects of a School Suicide Postvention Program. A Case Example, *Crisis, 17,* pp. 108-115, 1996.

42. R. Goldney and A. Berman, Postvention in Schools: Affective or Effective? *Crisis, 17,* pp. 98-99, 1996.
43. K. Johnson, *Trauma in the Lives of Children,* Hunter House, Claremont, California, 1989.
44. H. Nagara, Children's Reactions to the Death of Important Objects: A Developmental Approach, *Psychoanalytic Study of the Child, 25,* pp. 360-400, 1970.
45. G. Green, J. Wilson, and J. Lindy, Conceptualizing Post-Traumatic Stress Disorders: A Psychosocial Framework, in *Trauma and Its Wake,* C. Figley (ed.), Brunner/Mazel, New York, pp. 53-69, 1985.
46. I. Orbach, *Children Who Don't Want to Live: Understanding and Treating the Suicidal Child,* Jossey-Bass, San Francisco, 1988.
47. C. Pfeffer, *The Suicidal Child,* Guilford, New York, 1986.
48. P. Hazell and T. Lewin, Postvention following Adolescent Suicide, *Suicide and Life-Threatening Behavior, 23,* pp. 101-109, 1993.
49. C. Garrison, P. Lewinsohn, F. Marsteller, J. Langhinrichsen, and I. Lann, The Assessment of Suicidal Behavior in Adolescents, *Suicide & Life-Threatening Behavior, 21,* pp. 217-230, 1991.
50. P. Lewinsohn, C. Garrison, J. Langhinrichsen, and F. Marsteller, *The Assessment of Suicidal Behavior in Adolescents: A Review of Scales Suitable for Epidemiological Clinical Research,* National Institute of Mental Health, Rockville, Maryland, 1989.
51. D. Shaffer, A. Garland, V. Vieland, M. Underwood, and C. Busner, Adolescent Suicide Attempters: Response to Suicide Prevention Programs, *Journal of the American Medical Association, 264,* pp. 3151-3155, 1990.
52. J. Kalafat and M. Elias, An Evaluation of a School-Based Suicide Awareness Intervention, *Suicide and Life-Threatening Behavior, 24,* pp. 224-233, 1994.

CHAPTER 11

Social Support of the Health Care Provider

Mary L. S. Vachon

Social support has been found to be an essential variable for coping with many of life's stressors including occupational stress [1]. Early in the hospice/palliative care movement, social support was identified as crucial to survival in the field and the existence of a good social support system was seen as one of the qualities of the ideal palliative care nurse [2]. "Although social support has many facets, a core dimension of it involves participating in a network of caring and reciprocal relationships with others and creating a sense of belonging and a reason for living that transcends one's individual self" [3, p. 22]. Dr. Dean Ornish, the researcher who found that lifestyle changes reversed coronary artery disease without drugs or surgery [4], has said that to his mind, the most important intervention of the study was not the finding that dietary and lifestyle changes caused significant improvements in health and well-being, but ". . . the healing power of love and intimacy, and the emotional and spiritual transformation that often result from these" [5, p. 2].

The enhanced love and intimacy of belonging to a support group doubled the longevity of women with metastatic breast cancer [6] and interviews with people who experienced remarkable recoveries from advanced cancer [7] found that the survivors spoke of "the power of enduring marriages, devoted friendship, selfless acts, and indestructible love" [7, p. 210]. The authors summarize studies showing that "the link between personal relationships and immune function . . . is one of the most robust findings in psychoneuroimmunology" [7, p. 210] and conclude that if people without strong social support become sicker, then strengthening loving and supportive ties may be a way of stimulating the immune system. "Love and intimacy are at a root of what makes us sick and what makes us well, what causes us sadness and what brings happiness, what makes us suffer and what leads to healing" [5, p. 3]. What, then, are the implications of these findings for health care providers seeking to optimize their own physical and mental health?

Several years ago I interviewed professional caregivers to the critically ill, dying, and bereaved about the stress they experienced dealing with the critically ill, dying, and bereaved and what helped them to cope with this stress [8]. Over and over again people spoke of the importance of their social support system—both personal and professional—as being both a major source of support as well as a major stressor. At a personal level, our families can give us much pleasure, but can certainly be a source of great angst and pain if things are not going well on the home front. At a professional level, our team-mates and other colleagues can be a major source of support, but can also be guilty of scapegoating, sabotage, seem to be unduly critical, or just generally cause us to have more stress than we need to experience in our daily work.

This chapter will draw on the literature on social support, as well as the author's personal experience of over 30 years of involvement as a clinician, researcher, and educator in the fields of psychosocial oncology, palliative care, bereavement, and occupational stress.

YOU NEED MORE THAN ONE SOURCE OF SUPPORT

A good social support system has many components. These include:

- Someone to listen to us, at home or at work;
- Technical appreciation from an expert who gives feedback about one's professional performance and appreciates what one is doing;
- Technical challenge from one or more colleagues who can challenge one's way of thinking and working; this may or may not be the same person who provides technical appreciation;
- Emotional support from someone at home, at work, or in one's friendship system who is there for you, with whom you don't have to pretend, who knows you well, and whose support is unconditional;
- Emotional challenge from someone at home, or at work, or in one's friendship system who can comfortably ask if you are doing everything that you can in particular situations; and
- Shared social reality—someone who shares similar values, views, priorities, and some aspects of one's social situation [9].

It is clear from the above list that it generally takes more than one person to have a good social support system. In a study of volunteers exposed to the rhino virus that causes the common cold, the subjects were assessed for participation in 12 different social relationships: spouse, parents, parents-in-law, children, other close family members, close neighbors, friends, workmates, school mates, fellow volunteers in charity or community work, members of groups without religious affiliations (social, recreational or professional), and members of religious groups. One point was given for each type of relationship in which the person spoke to another person at least once every two weeks. The number of social relationships played a powerful role in protecting people from getting a cold. Those with only one to three types of relationships had more than four times the risk of getting the cold than those with six or more relationships. Those having four to five types of relationships had an intermediate risk. The differences in vulnerability to colds were not explained by antibody titers, smoking, exercise, amount of sleep, alcohol, vitamin C, or other factors [5, p. 62, quoting 10].

Participation in religious activity, one of the above social relationships, has been associated with decreased mortality in a number of studies [11]. While the reasons for this association are not clear, it is hypothesized that religious activity may be associated with improved health practices, improvements in social support, and marital-family stability.

PERSONAL SUPPORT SYSTEMS

Our support systems generally start on the home front with family and friends. It can make a big difference in one's ability to cope with work stressors if those at home are supportive. However, a professional caregiver's social support system may change over time. While initially family members and friends may be useful in helping the neophyte practitioner to debrief, over time caregivers turn more to colleagues who are better able to understand the specific stressors to which one is exposed [12, 13].

When Greek nurses working with dying children in oncology and critical care were compared [14], it was found that when the nurses were first hired they turned to family members and/or friends to discuss their work experiences and share their feelings. They learned quickly, however, that their friends and relatives found it difficult to listen to these accounts. In addition, as caregivers grow and mature, so too will the members of his/her support system. They may no longer want to play the support role [13, 15].

The role of family and friends in supporting caregivers has been found to be important but to have limits [8]. When caregivers working in HIV and oncology were compared, it was found that one-third of staff without long-term emotional relationships felt that their work kept them from being involved in such relationships. Most subjects reported spending a considerable amount of time discussing their work with partners. Thirty-nine percent reported that their partners complained regularly about their commitment to work and one-quarter reported that their relationship had suffered as a result of their work in oncology or HIV. While friends and family of HIV staff were more supportive of their working in the field, friends and family of oncology staff were more supportive of their actual work [16, 17].

SOCIAL SUPPORT AT WORK

Support from colleagues has been found to be very important for dealing with work-related stress [8]. High levels of mental ill health in hospice nurses were predicted by a lack of social support [18]. A comparison of hospice and oncology nurses showed that hospice nurses had significantly lower burnout scores than oncology nurses caring for the terminally ill on hospital-based oncology units [19]. The hospice nurses perceived a greater opportunity to express work-related feelings and to discuss problems in the workplace. A positive relationship was noted between perceived social support at work and lower burnout scores. Sixty-seven percent of palliative care nurses used "talking things over with a colleague" as a coping mechanism compared with 18 percent who talked with people at home [12].

Feelings of depression, grief, and guilt were found to be one of the major manifestations of stress in caregivers in many specialties. While some of these feelings were associated with grief related to the death of patients, some of the depression and grief was due to feelings of loss of self-esteem and not feeling supported by colleagues [8]. Self-esteem, the assessment of one's worth, is a resource that contributes strongly to the maintenance of one's identity [20, 21]. Self-esteem and a sense of mastery have been shown to be effective in sustaining staff against the emotional distress associated with hospice work [22, 23]. When the work situation undermines one's sense of self-esteem, the stage is set for problems with depression unless one has other resources that enable one to understand that the problems lie not with oneself, but with aspects of the work environment.

Papadatou and colleagues studied pediatric nurses in oncology and critical care and found that over time relationships with colleagues became progressively more important, and for some nurses this was their only source of emotional support [14]. There was an intimacy that evolved involving friendships and quasi-family relationships outside of work and even marriage. The support in that group of nurses was sought at four levels: informational, clinical/practical, emotional, and meaning making. The first two levels of support primarily benefited the patient; the latter two levels of support helped the nurses cope with the dying process and the death of children. There were similarities and differences in the levels of support used by both groups. Both groups valued *informational support*, although in different ways. Critical care nurses preferred information addressing clinical issues, while oncology nurses valued information exchange about the progress and treatment of individual patients and about acquiring new scientific knowledge. Both groups had difficulty with clinical/practical support to be discussed below.

The two groups were different in the receipt of *emotional support.* In the ICU the ongoing presence of several colleagues provided emotional and clinical support, while the pediatric oncology nurses were more apt to be without a colleague or physician at night. The oncology nurses were more apt to share emotions and experiences openly when a child died, whereas the ICU nurses shared primarily in small groups or with "friends." They tended to try to avoid focusing on issues of death and to focus their energy on saving other children.

Both groups found *meaning* in their work, but this also differed. The ICU nurses tended to feel "we lost this one, but others also need our care and help." Oncology nurses tended to invest their work with meaning by dealing with issues that would lead to a good and peaceful death. The meaning of their work aimed at comfort and dignity instead of cure (adapted from [17]).

PROBLEMS IN THE TEAM

In studies of caregivers to the critically ill and dying, organizational factors, such as personality issues and team conflict, were more commonly reported stressors than were problems in dealing with patients and families and issues related to death and dying [8, 24]. This finding has recently been replicated in a group of oncology nurses [25]. Organizational Factors and Coworker stress was rated as the most frequent and most intense stress cluster.

The environments in which teams work can produce uncertainty, anxiety, and frustration. The inability to manage these feelings can lead to a downward spiral with more anxiety and poorer job performance. If teams can learn to communicate, support one another, and problem solve, the results will be self-renewing or autotheraputic. If they fail to communicate and support one another, there will be more anxiety, which will drain team energy and spirit and lead to a negative downward spiral [26].

In a Finnish study of the ethical dilemmas confronting patients, physicians, and nurses in the context of incurable cancer, it was found that the doctors and nurses were not communicating with each other and there was a lack of cooperation between the two groups in decision-making situations [27]. Doctors talked primarily with one another and with patients. The nurses, as well as some of the physicians, said that it would be important to exchange views and opinions on treatments.

In the Greek study referred to above, there were also communication problems among colleagues in both the pediatric oncology and ICU groups [14]. There was dissatisfaction with the level of *clinical/practical support,* primarily because of difficulty in cooperation among team members. In oncology this involved difficulties with role blurring between physicians and nurses; in the ICU it involved rivalry and closed subgroups due to educational differences.

In a group of palliative care physicians, good relationships with staff were a major source of job satisfaction; however, encountering problems in relationships with nurses was the only aspect of work in which they had more difficulties than their colleagues in other specialties [28]. Part of the reason for this difficulty in communication may have been the increase in the number of palliative care physicians in the few years before this study. Previously, nurses in the United Kingdom had a major role in palliative care. With the increased number of palliative care medical specialists, the role of the nurses changed, their decision-making responsibilities were narrowed, and role dissatisfaction increased. The lack of participation in planning and decision-making that may develop out of poor staff relationships has been associated with depression and increased stress in palliative care staff [18, 29, 30].

Rivalry and anger often surface in team relationships. Many teams have difficulty dealing directly with anger and may use a variety of obstructive behaviors. These may involve *careerism and negative rivalry*—by concentrating on personal achievement and advancement, some team members' competitive instincts and energies may be channeled into rivalry among colleagues rather than on teamwork and effective patient care. Illusions of grandeur and interpersonal tugs of war occur on some teams where actual collaboration is low and mutual suspicion and antagonism is high. "Many team members engage in tugs-of-war, have territorial disputes, and play one-upmanship, sabotage one another's programs, cut one another's throats, while all the time proclaiming what a great team they are" [31]. *Lack of cooperation and discipline* occurs when teams have coordination without cooperation; they will go only so far. If team members are ordered about without consultation or participation, they will not give their best effort and will fail [17, 32].

The need to work through team dynamics and decision-making is crucial and often not easy. A quotation attributed to Dr. Cicely Saunders in the early days of the hospice movement, "If you say you work in a hospice team, you have to be willing to show your battle scars," is still true today.

WHAT WORKS?

Organizational Coping Mechanisms

Team Philosophy, Team Building, and Support

While the team was seen as one of the biggest stressors in the workplace and the place where stress was often manifest, teamwork was also mentioned as one of the major coping mechanisms for staff in most specialties [8]. Effective teamwork involved belonging to a team that knew what it was doing (team philosophy), knew how to get team members to work toward defined professional and personal goals (team building), and knew how to support one another through professional and personal stressors (team support).

> Effective teams: define the role of a "good team member" on that particular team; develop clear role definitions for team members; have the ability to share competencies; are educated together and communicate effectively together, including being able to deal with disagreement and anger in a constructive manner [8].

When palliative care staff were compared with those in other specialties, it was found that team philosophy, team building, and team support was the primary coping mechanism of palliative care workers and team conflict was less of a stressor than it was in other specialties [1, 8]. A relationship between these two findings was suggested, reflecting that the work hospice caregivers had put into team building, since the inception of the specialty, might have been responsible for the fact that the hospice team served more effectively to buffer the other stressors caregivers confronted than was the case in other specialties [1].

The development of supportive, collaborative work relationships may be fundamental to the enhancement of self-efficacy and self-esteem. Regular team meetings have been found to be important [33]. Such meetings served to set goals to accomplish the work of the team, provided a time of evaluation and reflection on the work being accomplished, and allowed for shared decision-making. It is important that organizations create the opportunity for ongoing support, and that staff have the time to attend support sessions, especially for those working alone in the community. This may consist of support through team meetings, easy access to consultants, a buddy or mentor system for ongoing support, and the opportunity to debrief after critical incidents [17].

Each setting must develop their own approach to dealing with team building and education. One such approach involved continuous education and an organization that stimulated the staff's own initiative but was also capable of supporting the staff when necessary [34]. Another setting used the concept of initiating educational meetings whenever there was an issue that caused difficulty for staff. The session allowed for an intellectual approach to dealing with the issue and would often then lead to discussions of a more personal nature [35].

While support groups are recommended almost as a panacea for either team stress or problems with patients, they were found in one study to be the least commonly mentioned organizational coping strategy [8]. Horowitz and colleagues reported on interdisciplinary "pizza rounds" held weekly on the Neurooncology Service at MSKCC [36]. The purpose of the rounds is to

> enhance patient care by improving interdisciplinary functioning and by providing staff with the opportunity to exchange ideas, solve problems involving difficult patients and families, develop consistent plans for patient management, and ventilate their emotional responses to job-related stress. Food is

> served as a means of increasing attendance and reducing hierarchical barriers between staff members [36, p. 330].

A social worker and psychiatrist lead the group. Although no formal evaluation of the meetings has been conducted, the authors feel that the fact that the group has endured for a period of years attests to its effectiveness.

Teams need to be able to effectively grieve for the deaths of those with whom they work. Memorial services, death rounds where team members can share what happened at the time of death, and reflect on the care given and lessons learned can be effective; Memory Books in which teams can reminiscence and reflect on patients who have died; grief and loss support groups; participating in memorial projects such as the AIDS Quilt Project; and journaling are but a few of the approaches which might prove to be useful. For staff that have lost many clients over a brief period of time, a shift from intensive patient contact to less intensive contact can be useful [37]. Work groups that develop norms for realistic goal-setting and limit setting can also be useful in helping caregivers [37]. Techniques that have been shown to be effective in helping staff to deal with multiple losses include:

- witness the pain—tell the story; express the pain to allow catharsis and healing;
- help the person to stay involved in something outside him/herself;
- assist to create meaningful rituals;
- provide structure and support when emotional flooding is overwhelming—utilize action instead of immobility and fear; and
- refocus on the elevating emotions of joy and hope [1, 38].

Tested, Tried, and True Methods of Coping

The above methods of coping at an organizational level have been shown to work in a variety of articles. In concluding this chapter the author offers a number of personal coping mechanisms related to social support that have helped her to cope effectively as she has worked in the fields of oncology, palliative care, bereavement, and occupational stress for over 30 years. These include:

- A spiritual life which connects the individual with the transcendent from which one can derive a sense of meaning and purpose in life which can be sustaining even when personal and professional stress is at a high level;
- A solid, supportive family system comprised of people who can listen, provide emotional support, emotional challenge, and practical assistance;
- A network of friends with whom one has reciprocal relationships comprised of persons who are involved in various aspects of one's personal and professional life, to whom one can turn for help in a variety of ways and who in turn can turn to you for such help;

- Supportive colleagues at work, whether those be team members; colleagues outside of one's direct team with whom one can share the trials, tribulations, and joys of the workplace; administrators who can understand the stress to which one is exposed;
- Colleagues with whom one may not work with but who understand one's professional trials and tribulations, with whom one can share a similar professional value system and from whom one can receive support. The author belongs to a support group of oncology nurses who have met every six weeks for 25 years. A group that shares personal and professional life experiences together such as this is of inestimable value;
- A community of others reflecting one's religious beliefs or value systems;
- A mentor or supervisor who can provide support and challenge and with whom ideally one can reflect over the years. For many years the author found it helpful to meet regularly with a psychiatrist to develop insight and to receive support in challenging situations. In recent social contacts it has been helpful to have her reflections on my personal development over the years. A diagnosis of cancer 4½ years ago led to a renewed interest in spirituality. Receiving supervision from colleagues as I have begun to integrate new insights into my clinical practice has been very valuable;
- An outside life which can sustain one if the work situation becomes particularly difficult; and
- Developing skills that make one "marketable" in situations outside of the present workplace in case a situation of person-environment misfit occurs.

The work we do is difficult to do in isolation. A multifaceted social support system can sustain us and enrich our ability to continue to do the work to which we feel drawn and called.

REFERENCES

1. M. L. S. Vachon, Staff Stress in Hospice/Palliative Care: A Review, *Palliative Medicine, 9,* pp. 91-122, 1995.
2. C. C. Gotay, S. Crockett, and C. West, Palliative Home Care Nursing: Nurses' Perceptions of Roles and Stress, *Canadian Mental Health, 33,* pp. 6-9, 1985.
3. D. G. Larson, *The Helper's Journey,* Research Press, Champaign, Illinois, 1993.
4. D. Ornish, *Dr. Dean Ornish's Program for Reversing Heart Disease,* Random House, Ballantine Books, New York, 1991.
5. D. Ornish, *Love and Survival: The Scientific Basis for the Healing Power of Intimacy,* HarperCollins, New York, 1998.
6. D. Spiegel, J. R. Bloom, H. C. Kraemer, and E. Gothic, Effects of Psychosocial Treatment on Survival of Women with Metastatic Breast Cancer, *The Lancet,* pp. 888-891, 1989.
7. C. Hirshberg and M. I. Barasch, *Remarkable Recovery,* Riverhead Books, New York, 1995.

8. M. L. S. Vachon, *Occupational Stress in the Care of the Critically Ill, the Dying and the Bereaved,* Hemisphere, New York, 1987.
9. A. M. Pines and E. Aronson, *Career Burnout: Causes and Cures,* Free Press, New York, 1988.
10. S. Cohen, Psychosocial Models of the Role of Social Support in the Etiology of Physical Disease, *Health Psychology, 7,* pp. 269-297, 1988.
11. M. E. McCullough, W. T. Hoyt, D. B. Larson, H. G. Koenig, and C. Thoresen, Religious Involvement and Mortality: A Meta-Analytic Review, *Health Psychology, 19,* pp. 211-222, 2000.
12. D. A. Alexander and E. Ritchie, 'Stressors' and Difficulties in Dealing with the Terminal Patient, *Journal of Palliative Care, 6*:3, pp. 28-33, 1990.
13. M. L. S. Vachon, Emotional Problems in Palliative Medicine: Patient, Family, and Professional, in *Oxford Textbook of Palliative Medicine,* D. Doyle, G. W. Hanks, and N. MacDonald (eds.), Oxford University Press, Oxford, pp. 577-605, 1993.
14. D. Papadatou, I. Papazoglou, D. Petraki, and T. Bellali, Mutual Support among Nurses Who Provide Care to Dying Children, *Illness, Crisis and Loss, 7,* pp. 37-48, 1999.
15. J. D. McCue, The Effects of Stress on Physicians and Their Medical Practice, *New England Journal of Medicine, 306,* pp. 458-463, 1982.
16. D. Miller and P. Gillies, Is There Life After Work? Experiences of HIV and Oncology Health Staff, *AIDS Care, 8,* pp. 167-182, 1996.
17. M. L. S. Vachon, The World of the Palliative Care Nurse, in *Oxford Textbook of Palliative Nursing,* B. Ferrell and N. Coyle (eds.), Oxford University Press, New York, pp. 647-662, 2000.
18. C. L. Cooper and S. Mitchell, Nursing the Critically Ill and Dying, *Human Relations, 43,* pp. 297-311, 1990.
19. P. J. Bram and L. F. Katz, Study of Burnout in Nurses Working in Hospice and Hospital Oncology Settings, *Oncology Nursing Forum, 16,* pp. 555-560, 1989.
20. L. I. Pearlin and C. Schooler, The Structure of Coping, *Journal of Health and Social Behavior, 19,* pp. 2-21, 1978.
21. L. I. Pearlin, M. A. Lieberman, E. G. Menahga, and J. T. Mullen, The Stress Process, *Journal of Health and Social Behavior, 22,* pp. 337-356, 1981.
22. R. Yancik, Sources of Work Stress for Hospice Staff, *Journal of Psychosocial Oncology, 2*:1, pp. 21-31, 1984.
23. R. Yancik, Coping with Hospice Work Stress, *Journal of Psychosocial Oncology, 2*:2, pp. 19-35, 1984.
24. A. Munley, Sources of Hospice Staff Stress and How to Cope with It, *Nursing Clinics of North America, 20,* pp. 343-355, 1985.
25. G. A. Florio, J. P. Donnelly, and M. A. Zevon, The Structure of Work-Related Stress and Coping among Oncology Nurses in High-Stress Medical Settings: A Transactional Analysis, *Journal of Occupational Health Psychology, 3,* pp. 227-242, 1998.
26. H. Wise, R. Beckhard, I. Rubin, and G. Kyte (eds.), *Making Health Care Teams Work,* Ballinger, Cambridge, Massachusetts, 1974.
27. M. Kuuppelomăki and S. Lauri, Ethical Dilemmas in the Care of Patients with Incurable Cancer, *Nursing Ethics, 5,* pp. 283-293, 1998.
28. J. Graham, A. J. Ramirez, A. Cull, W. M. Gregory, I. Finlay, A. Hoy, and M. A. Richards, Job Stress and Satisfaction among Palliative Physicians: A CRC/ICRF Study, *Palliative Medicine, 10,* pp. 185-194, 1996.

29. G. Hart, P. Yates, M. Clinton, and C. Windsor, Mediating Conflict and Control: Practice Challenges for Nurses Working in Palliative Care, *International Journal of Nursing Studies, 35,* pp. 252-258, 1998.
30. D. A. Alexander and M. MacLeod, Stress among Palliative Care Matrons: A Major Problem for a Minority Group, *Palliative Medicine, 6,* pp. 111-124, 1992.
31. D. Heming, The Titanic Triumvirate: Teams, Teamwork and Teambuilding, *Canadian Journal of Occupational Therapy, 55,* pp. 15-20, 1988.
32. M. L. S. Vachon, What Makes a Team? *Palliative Care Today, 5*:3, pp. 34-35, 1996.
33. H. Woolley, A. Stein, G. C. Forrest, and J. D. Baum, Staff Stress and Job Satisfaction at a Children's Hospice, *Archives of Diseases of Children, 64,* pp. 114-118, 1989.
34. B. Beck-Friis, P. Strang, and P.-O. Sjoden, Caring for Severely Ill Cancer Patients: A Comparison of Working Conditions in Hospital-Based Home Care and In Hospital, *Supportive Care in Cancer, 1,* pp. 145-151, 1993.
35. E. Bruera, Personal communication, 1994.
36. S. A. Horowitz, S. D. Passik, M. Brish, and W. S. Breitbart, *Psycho-Oncology, 3,* pp. 329-332, 1994.
37. M. E. Killeen, Getting Through Our Grief: For Caregivers of Persons with AIDS, *American Journal of Hospice and Palliative Care, 10*:5, pp. 18-24, 1993.
38. T. Grothe and L. McKusick, Coping with Multiple Loss, *Focus, 7*:7, pp. 5-6, 1992.

CHAPTER 12

Structural Issues in Support

Elizabeth Slump

It has long been known that the isolation of an individual or groups of individuals further adds to their anxiety and despair. In fact, isolation impedes the process of socialization and indeed may prevent socialization from either taking place at all or happening in a negative form, which in itself sets up a potential problem in the future.

Social support of the suicidal is imperative in order that the individual can cope with their immense burden of hopelessness, anxiety, fear, depression, sense of failure, and anger. Social support is essential for those socially isolated individuals who become suicidal because they do not see any hope to ease their depression and their loneliness. Social support of the suicidal is crucial for the maintenance of an effective prevention program. Those who are bereft by suicide require social support immediately after the suicide and usually for some time after. Unfortunately, in our society, where time is a precious and sought after resource, that support may be sporadic at best.

Social support includes doing something about the ills of unemployment, divorce, homelessness, poor and inadequate parenting, neglect of the mentally ill, neglect of the elderly, medical care services pushed to inadequacy, social services loaded with cases, violence, and loss of spiritual values.

Professionals doing counseling and therapy with suicidal individuals must acquaint themselves with the ills which exist in our society and be prepared to help clients find their way through systems which are often heavy with bureaucracy and too burdened with needy clients. Large numbers of needy clients often mean that the individual needs of a suicidal client do not receive the kind of attention necessary to dispel, at least partially, some of the hopelessness, anxiety and sense of failure often felt by the client.

A resourceful counselor or therapist can help an unemployed client by providing suggestions where they may seek some employment. They can show the client how to research areas where they might work. The counselor can often make inquiries to a potential employer and provide support to help the client adjust to the new situation and to the potential anxiety which may arise from the new adjustment situation.

Poor and inadequate parenting as well as divorce in our society is causing pain for young people. Many community agencies provide training in parenting skills and our high schools provide parenting courses and courses on controversial family issues such as relationships and marriage and family. Unfortunately, more young people need to study those areas in our schools. Our governments must focus more on training in these areas with money to develop more training of young educators in an effort to better equip them to handle these issues in our schools. More effective parenting and more emphasis on the values of home and family could also result in fewer young people opting to live on the streets. The homeless need to be encouraged to stay in their homes and thus avoid the lifestyles which result in despair, anxiety, hopelessness, and a life of hardship and suffering.

The mentally ill are of great concern and it seems as if more and more of them are treated medically then released prematurely, even when suicidal, because there is no room for them in crowded hospitals. Only the severely mentally ill are hospitalized, the remainder sent home or to the streets, some of them suicidal, a danger to themselves and possibly to society. Professionals dealing with a mentally ill client who is suicidal must keep the lines of communication open, must be able to establish rapport with the client, and able to set up a support network who can help the client learn to cope and survive. This is a difficult task and requires much more time than most professionals have to deal with the client. Finding and involving a social support system can make a difference in the life of the individual while developing some self-worth and helping to eliminate fear and anxiety.

Neglect of the elderly has risen to our consciousness and has become one of the most shocking ills of our society. More and more of our population is becoming older and it is inevitable that more aging and elderly will have to leave their homes and move to elder care. Some elderly are living in care facilities that are inadequate in their ability to provide social support and the result is that some aging and elderly are socially isolated. Suicide rates among the elderly are higher than we should expect and climbing gradually. Many of our aging and elderly are suffering from depression and anxiety often forgotten or abandoned by the families they lovingly reared. There are many ways a social support system can help our aged. Visits from friends, acquaintances, church groups, pastoral care teams, service clubs, sports teams, public figures, and children can help so much to ease the loneliness and despair. There are community activities and events where these people can be taken for outings where they can see and meet new people. Schools can and should take this as an opportunity for a school project. This could be a grandparenting project where young people are matched with a resident of a nursing home. There could be visits to the resident and the student could do creative projects with the resident, take them for short walks, and call them from their homes to chat with the resident grandparent. The young people would learn from these older people and the aged are included in some activities where they feel a valued member of society. This program has had huge success in those schools and homes for the aged. It requires a lot of initial organization but the benefits to all involved are worth the effort.

It is a huge task to try to correct the social ills developing from our stressed medical and social services systems. These services are pushed to the limit and can only provide minimum social support for the suicidal. There are resources needed for a prevention and treatment center for each large urban area. This facility, in addition to providing counseling and therapy, could provide a support network that could utilize community volunteers as supports for the suicidal. Our provincial health departments must seriously look at this option. Professionals who do suicide prevention and intervention must lobby the governments to provide this type of service since there is so little there to help the suicidal. This could in turn take some strain off the hospital psychiatric services. This in fact could result in huge savings economically.

The past three years have been filled with violence and in spite of the resources used in an effort to reduce violence there is an abundance in our schools, in our communities, and in our families.

Professionals can be proactive and resourceful where violent acts and bullying can affect the well-being of our young. Bullying in our schools has had an impact on young people, particularly those who may be suicidal. More time must be spent talking to kids and helping them deal with less than ideal home situations. Spending time communicating with kids, involving them in projects designed to build self-esteem, and recognizing their successes are helpful initiatives.

Spiritual values are lacking in many people today. A professional can help to develop some idea of spiritual values or do much to restore ones long marred by failure and hopelessness. Treating the suicidal client with love and compassion and care is hard work. It requires consistency of support, learning to deal with setbacks, and a belief in the combination of mind, body, and spirit. A highly effective treatment includes the establishment of rapport and fostering the rapport with love and compassion to accomplish trust with the client and support for them. Those with strong spiritual values are often able to provide strong support.

The plight of Canadian Innui in Northern Labrador and natives in Northern Ontario is a current concern. The suicide rate among the young in these communities is currently the highest in the world. The recent rash of suicides among the young in these communities has received international attention. Social support for these peoples should include helping them to maintain their language and family patterns. They also need support to develop parenting skills, life skills management, and suicide prevention programs. Their suicidal young need encouragement, to be taught coping skills and the development of self-esteem. They need to know that they are valuable to the country for the diversity they contribute. A carefully designed program including an ongoing maintenance element delivered by a team of compassionate knowledgeable professionals would help establish stability among these peoples.

Social support for the suicidal is crucial for the maintenance of an effective prevention program. This support could prevent a potential suicide before it is known that an individual is at risk. If there is a support system of caring individuals to help those who live alone without family near them, this could quell suicidal feelings and give the individual the hope to carry on.

> Kyle was a sixteen year old who stayed alone and was called a loner by many students. He had difficulties with other students. One day he asked me for some books about suicide. An assessment was done after he indicated that he wanted to talk to me. This assessment indicated that Kyle was very depressed and desperate for help. A treatment plan was set up for him but this plan included social support for Kyle. He was included in school trips and was encouraged to get involved with students in his classes. I visited him at his grandparent's home and helped him with schoolwork. There were contacts to his teachers to help them understand his plight. There were invitations to church activities where he met a clergy person who involved him and talked with him. There were successful efforts to help him decide what his educational goals were and a plan to help him reach those goals. Kyle had a solid social support system that aided the prevention program set for him by the therapist. Kyle eventually moved on and became less suicidal, finishing college and presently is a husband and father with a good job and self-esteem. He credits his success with the prevention but also to the support he received from so many caring people.

This case can also provide ideas of support for those widowed, divorced, aging, ill, and lonely individuals who have little or no support in their community. Taking the time to call, drop in to visit, offer to help prepare a meal, or doing things like inviting them to a meal at your home or a social function are ways of showing some concern and will help the lonely individual.

The social support of the client can be as effective as the treatment plan. The suicidal needs a prevention plan in which rapport and trust are vital. Part of the plan should include a non-suicide contract that relies strongly on the commitment from the professional and the suicidal. Social support from family, friends, community, social services—those individuals making sure the suicidal is not alone—are invaluable in any prevention plan. What seems trivial to us can be overwhelming, but helping the client to do chores and errands can let them know we care. Drop in visits, phone calls, taking them to social events, movies, or the corner restaurant allow them some diversion and can give feelings of comfort and support for the suicidal. An effective prevention plan requires dedication to the suicidal and connecting to the individual frequently. An effective social support system can greatly augment the prevention program.

Those bereft by suicide are of concern to professionals and families because they receive love and care immediately following the suicide but after a time they tend to be neglected. Suicide being the tragedy it is, often leaves survivors stunned and feeling powerful emotions. Social support is vital to helping a family to reach some level of resolution. It is just so tough for some individuals to cope with each hour of each day, and the notes of support, phone calls, and kindness all help to cope. Those providing social support should provide opportunities for those bereft to tell their story and talk about their emotions. Answers are not necessary, just listen and stay away from trying to provide answers. Encourage the bereft to keep a journal describing their feelings. Give them a chance to express their anger as you listen. Include these survivors in activities where they may meet people who are understanding and compassionate. Support groups for those bereft by suicide are invaluable for a community. They provide an outlet to verbalize feelings, receive support, and where the bereft can learn to deal with any shame or stigma which may be attached to their loved one's suicide. In addition to feelings of anger, shame, or guilt the bereft may feel responsible for the suicide and that they should have prevented the death. Listening to the bereft and encouraging them to talk about these concerns helps them to come to terms with the feelings. All support must be reassuring, not judgmental or try to answer the "why" questions. In some communities there is an attempt to hide suicide as the cause of death. When it is known that the cause of death was suicide, support from close friends and family is necessary on a daily basis so those bereft can begin to cope. Even the easiest and simplest tasks of surviving can be overwhelming for individuals dealing with the suicide of a loved one.

There is no question that social support to the suicidal is crucial. Our young Canadian natives in Northern Labrador and Northern Ontario, our young people in our towns and cities, our aging and elderly in their homes, and all those bereft by suicide need kind, caring, and enduring support as they deal with the devastating tragedy of suicide. This support may need to be ongoing for a longer period of time than the support for other kinds of deaths but those giving the support and helping in ways they never know and will make a difference. It seems that since our society has grown and changed that so too has our approach to helping those in need. We need to examine ways that we can be a support system to those in pain. Often it is not convenient to try to give some social support but individually in our communities we can volunteer our skills, our knowledge, and our kindness to try to help what is done by our stressed medical system. Social support networks could save some individuals a lot of pain and can save lives as well. These networks have the potential to take some stress away from a healthcare system burdened with new demands and increasingly fewer resources with which to deal with these demands.

Contributors

CAROL H. EHRLICH, Ph.D., Chairperson Emerita of the Department of Audiology and Speech Pathology, Children's Hospital, Denver, and former Assistant Professor at the University of Denver, Columbia University College of Physicians and Surgeons, and Colorado State University, became a Fellow of the American Speech-Language-Hearing Association in 1983. She has written numerous articles for journals and magazines, chapters in several books, and is co-author of *All Kinds of Love: Experiencing Hospice* (Baywood Publishing Company, Amityville, New York, 1997)

THOMAS GOLDEN, LCSW, is well known in the field of healing from loss. Tom's book *Swallowed by a Snake: The Gift of the Masculine Side of Healing* has been acclaimed by Elisabeth Kübler-Ross and others. Tom enjoys presenting workshops in the United States, Canada, and Australia, having been named the "1999 International Grief Educator" by the Australian Centre for Grief Education. His workshops are known to be entertaining and informative. Tom brings a gentle sense of humor and a gift for storytelling as he draws on his 25 years of practical, hands-on clinical experience. His work has been featured in *The New York Times, The Washington Post,* and *U.S. News and World Report,* as well as on CNN and CBS Evening News. For information on workshops Tom can be reached at his award winning website webhealing.com or by phone 1-301-670-1027.

MINDY L. K. GOUGH obtained her B.S.W. and a Certificate in Palliative Care and Thanatology from the University of Western Ontario. She has a private practice called A Gentle Place for Grieving Children.

RABBI EARL A. GROLLMAN, D.H.L., D.D., is a pioneer in the field of crisis intervention, the author of 26 books, and he lectures extensively around the world. His latest volume is *Living with Loss, Healing with Hope: A Jewish Perspective* (Beacon Press, Boston, Massachusetts).

ROSE MARIE JACO is Professor Emerita of Social Work at King's College in London, Ontario. In addition she has a private practice as a family practitioner in London, Ontario. Dr. Jaco has been quite active in social services in southwest Ontario. At present she sits on the boards of several agencies, including the London Interfaith Counseling Centre, an organization she was instrumental in founding.

CAROLYN JAFFE, R.N., D.H.L., retired primary care hospice nurse, has been Nursing Representative for the National Hospice Organization. She won the Florence Nightingale award from the University of Colorado in 1990 for her contributions to health care in Colorado, and in 1995 was named a Doctor of Humane Letters by the University of Denver. She is co-author of *All Kinds of Love: Experiencing Hospice* (Baywood Publishing Company, Amityville, New York, 1997)

ANTOON A. LEENAARS is a registered psychologist in private practice in Windsor, Canada, and a member of the Faculty at the University of Leiden, The Netherlands. He was the first Past President of the Canadian Association for Suicide Prevention (CASP), and is a past President of the American Association of Suicidology (AAS). He has collaborated with over 50 colleagues in 20 nations, and has published over 100 professional articles/chapters on suicide, trauma, homicide, gun control, and related issues. He has published 10 books, most recently *Lives and Deaths: Selections from the Works of Edwin S. Shneidman,* and is Editor-in-Chief of *Suicide Studies* (formerly, *Archives of Suicide Research*). Dr. Leenaars is a recipient of both CASP's Research Award and the AAS's Shneidman Award for outstanding contribution in research in suicidology. He is recognized for his international efforts in suicide prevention and has served as an expert witness in legal cases dealing with wrongful death, suicide, and homicide.

DAVID LESTER has Ph.D. degrees from Brandeis University (United States) in psychology and Cambridge University (United Kingdom) in social and political science. He was President of the International Association for Suicide Prevention and is currently Professor of Psychology at the Richard Stockton College of New Jersey. He has written extensively on thanatology and, especially, suicidal behavior.

JOHN D. MORGAN, Ph.D. is a pioneer in the death awareness movement. Dr. John D. (Jack) Morgan has written about a wide range of topics in the field of death and bereavement, drawn from his work as educator, author, lecturer, and program organizer. In 1997 he received an award from the Association for Death Education and Counseling for his work in Death Education. Born in San Francisco, and holding a doctorate from the University of Southern California, Jack has resided in Canada since 1963.

DARCY NICHOLS worked for over 15 years with cancer patients and their families as an oncology/hospice nurse in the United States. She now teaches in the Thanatology Program at King's College in London, Ontario, Canada and has a private practice in counseling specializing in bereavement-related issues. She is also a well-known author and lecturer on topics important to professional caregivers and bereaved individuals.

MARIE-ANTOINETTE PARISIO has more than 20 years experience in working with adults with developmental disabilities in the L'Arche communities. She has experience with them in different cultural backgrounds: France, The Middle East, and Canada. For three years now she has been the Community Leader and Director of the L'Arche community in London, Ontario. She has a certificate in Palliative Care and Thanatology from the University of Western Ontario. She continues to be intrigued and challenged by the little research and resources available on death, dying, and grief for adults with developmental disabilities. Often she witnessed complicated grief in that very disenfranchised population. However, she also witnessed the Transformative power of grief work in the same population when people are recognized the right to grief and are offered the necessary support to do so. This grief support group manual could be one of the tools to help adults with developmental disabilities do some of their grief work.

ELIZABETH SLUMP is a Death Educator, Grief Therapist, and Sociologist in private practice in Ottawa, Ontario, Canada. In addition to counseling, Elizabeth does consulting to Employee Assistance providers, business, industry, and education where she does training in workplace grief and loss and handling grief and loss in the school environment. A former high school educator, Elizabeth Slump has worked for many years in suicide prevention and postvention counseling and developing school programs. She is a member of A.D.EC., O.A.C.C.P.P. C.A.C. and B.O.N and she is a frequent speaker at conferences and community service organizations.

ROBERT G. STEVENSON has been an educator for over 30 years. He currently works in a residential alcohol/drug rehabilitation program and teaches graduate counseling courses at Mercy College in New York. He has published over 60 articles on loss and grief in professional journals and texts and has edited four books of his own. He is an active member of both the International Work Group on Death, Dying, and Bereavement (I.W.G.) and the Association for Death Education and Counseling (A.D.E.C.). He is a graduate of the College of the Holy Cross (BA) and holds master's degrees from Fairleigh Dickinson University (M.A.T.), Montclair State University (MA), and a doctorate from Fairleigh Dickinson (Ed.D.). He is nationally certified by the Association for Death Education and Counseling as a death educator and grief counselor, has served on their board of directors and as chairman of their Education Institute, and on their board of certification review. Dr. Stevenson has written curricula for social studies, health, and death education and has been honored for his work as an educator and counselor by: The New Jersey Professional Counselors' Association, the New Jersey Governor's Office, the Best Practice Awards of the New Jersey Department of Education, New Jersey School Boards' Association, United States Chess Federation, and the National Council for the Social Studies. He is listed in *Who's Who Among America's Teachers, Who's Who Among Human Service Professionals,* and *Who's Who Among International Authors.* He was the recipient of the 1997 Wendel Williams Outstanding Teacher Award and the 1993 ADEC Death Educator Award for his contributions to those fields.

MARY L. S. VACHON is a nurse, clinical sociologist, psychotherapist, researcher, and educator living in Toronto, Canada. She is Associate Professor in the Departments of Psychiatry and Public Health Sciences at the University of

Toronto, a psychotherapist and consultant in private practice, and Clinical Consultant at Wellspring, a community-based program for people with cancer. She was previously employed at Massachusetts General Hospital, the Clarke Institute of Psychiatry, and Sunnybrook and Women's College Health Sciences Centre. She has published widely, lectured throughout much of the world, and is the recipient of many awards. Most recently she was named the Distinguished Scientist of 2001 by the National Hospice and Palliative Care Organization.

SUSANNE WENCKSTERN, M.A., C.Psych. Assoc., is with the Psychological Services staff at the Greater Essex County District School Board, Canada. She is one of Canada's leading researchers, being a co-editor of the national volume *Suicide in Canada.* She was Secretary for the Canadian Association for Suicide Prevention (CASP). Her publications include, with A. Leenaars, *Suicide Prevention in Schools.* She is senior editor of the national handbook *Suicide Prevention in Canadian Schools,* and is a recognized national and international trainer in suicide prevention with youth. Susanne Wenckstern has received CASP's Service Award for outstanding leadership in community services in suicide prevention.

Index